P9-CRC-300

# THE BOMBING OF PEARL HARBOR

# THE BOMBING OF PEARL HARBOR

ESSENTIAL LIBRARY OF
## WORLD WAR II

BY SUE BRADFORD EDWARDS

CONTENT CONSULTANT

PETER VERMILYEA
WESTERN CONNECTICUT STATE UNIVERSITY

Essential Library

An Imprint of Abdo Publishing
abdopublishing.com

abdopublishing.com

Published by Abdo Publishing, a division of ABDO, PO Box 398166, Minneapolis, Minnesota 55439. Copyright © 2016 by Abdo Consulting Group, Inc. International copyrights reserved in all countries. No part of this book may be reproduced in any form without written permission from the publisher. Essential Library™ is a trademark and logo of Abdo Publishing.

Printed in the United States of America, North Mankato, Minnesota

052015
092015

THIS BOOK CONTAINS
RECYCLED MATERIALS

Cover Photos: Corbis
Interior Photos: Corbis, 1, 3; US National Archives and Records Administration, 6, 72 (top left), 73 (top right), 73 (bottom right), 82, 95, 98 (bottom); US Naval History and Heritage Command, 9, 55, 57, 72 (right); Army Signal Corps Collection/US National Archives and Records Administration/US Naval History and Heritage Command, 10, 71; Bettmann/Corbis, 16, 27, 46, 49, 74, 99 (top); AP Images, 19, 21, 23, 41, 42, 67, 89, 91, 98 (top); Shizuo Fukui/Kure Maritime Museum, 29; Kure Maritime Museum, 31; US Navy/US National Archives and Records Administration/US Naval History and Heritage Command, 33, 52, 59, 62, 72 (bottom left); Kingendai/AFLO/Nippon News/Corbis, 35; Hulton-Deutsch Collection/Corbis, 38; US Marine Corps History Division, 50, 69, 78, 99 (bottom); Eiicha Tanaka/AP Images, 61; Library of Congress, 65; US Navy/US National Archives and Records Administration, 73 (left); US Army Signal Corps/Library of Congress, 77, 81; Robert Kradin/AP Images, 84; Harris & Ewing/Library of Congress, 93

Editor: Nick Rebman
Series Designers: Kelsey Oseid and Maggie Villaume

Library of Congress Control Number: 2015930963
Cataloging-in-Publication Data

Edwards, Sue Bradford.
 The bombing of Pearl Harbor / Sue Bradford Edwards.
  p. cm. -- (Essential library of World War II)
Includes bibliographical references and index.
ISBN 978-1-62403-791-7
1. Pearl Harbor (Hawaii), Attack on, 1941--Juvenile literature.  2. World War, 1939-1945--Hawaii--Juvenile literature.   I. Title.
940.54/26693--dc23

2015930963

# CONTENTS

CHAPTER 1    WAR COMES TO THE UNITED STATES ...................... 6

CHAPTER 2    GLOBAL UNREST ......................................16

CHAPTER 3    JAPAN'S PLAN .......................................28

CHAPTER 4    LIMITED INTELLIGENCE ...............................42

CHAPTER 5    SUBMARINES .........................................52

CHAPTER 6    THE FIRST WAVE OF AIRCRAFT.........................62

CHAPTER 7    THE SECOND WAVE OF AIRCRAFT .......................74

CHAPTER 8    THE AFTERMATH .....................................84

TIMELINE ....................................98
ESSENTIAL FACTS.............................100
GLOSSARY ...................................102
ADDITIONAL RESOURCES........................104
SOURCE NOTES................................106
INDEX.......................................110
ABOUT THE AUTHOR............................112

# WAR COMES TO THE UNITED STATES

On the evening of December 6, 1941, 15-year-old Martin Matthews presented an officer with his pass from Ford Island Naval Air Station. Matthews was a seaman first class, and his pass showed he had several days of leave from his post at the base. With the officer's approval, Matthews followed his friend, Seaman First Class William Stafford, aboard the USS *Arizona*. The ship was stationed in Pearl Harbor, just outside Honolulu, Hawaii.

The two bunked down for the night in Stafford's compartment and got up at 6:00 a.m. They donned their dress whites and reported to the mess for breakfast. After they ate, Stafford agreed to show Matthews around the *Arizona*. "I wish I could get duty aboard a battleship," Matthews said.[1]

Matthews heard a noise and looked to the right, where he spotted aircraft flying toward the ship. He heard a thundering noise and then saw fire and dirt flying up beneath the planes. He thought he was seeing one of the scheduled gunnery practices for the soldiers and sailors who were training in and around Pearl Harbor.

Then an alarm sounded on the *Arizona*, and Stafford ran to report to his duty station. Each sailor had an assigned job in a specific location. They prepared the ship to fight the attackers—the Japanese. Matthews stayed toward the back of the ship because he did not have a job or the training to know what to do.

The *Arizona* was hit sometime between 8:30 and 8:45 a.m., when an explosion thundered on the right side of the ship. Matthews saw flames, and the ship shuddered beneath his feet as he watched the men try to get the guns ready to fire.

The gunners had to get the ammunition out of locked storage, but the person in charge of the locker would not unlock it without the permission of the officer of the day. In the confusion of planes firing and dropping torpedoes, the men

## TEENS IN THE NAVY?

Recruits had to be 17 years old to join the US military, but Martin Matthews entered the navy at only 15 years of age. If a military recruiter thought someone like Matthews looked too young, he would ask the recruit's parents to sign a legal paper called an affidavit. Because Matthews's father signed an affidavit saying his son was 17 years old, Matthews was able to join the navy. He was stationed at Ford Island Naval Air Station in Pearl Harbor. While there, he attended aviation metal craft school and learned to repair damaged aircraft.

Japanese planes began their attack on Battleship Row on the morning of December 7, 1941.

Sailors rescue a survivor as the USS *West Virginia* burns.

did not know where this officer was, so one sailor broke the locker open with a metal tool.

As the Japanese planes dropped bombs, several hit the *Arizona*. Matthews ended up in the sea, but later he could not remember whether he had jumped or been blown overboard. Once he was in the water, he swam away from the ship toward the closest mooring buoy.

The buoy was approximately 25 yards (23 m) from the *Arizona*, and Matthews hung on to the far side, keeping it between himself and the ship. He watched as Japanese planes attacked the US ships in the harbor and the aircraft on Ford Island.

As the battle raged, steel, pieces of wood, fire, and even body parts rained into the water around Matthews. Eventually, a series of explosions went off aboard the *Arizona*. Matthews watched as the final blast lifted the middle of the battleship up in the water. Then the ship buckled and, as water poured through the broken hull, the *Arizona* settled on the bottom of the shallow harbor. It came to rest with the bridge, from which the captain commanded the ship, still above water level.

Matthews left the algae-covered buoy and swam nearly a mile (1.6 km) through water covered in oil and diesel fuel. When he crawled onto the beach

## DAWN ATTACK

The Japanese knew the best time to attack Pearl Harbor would be at dawn on a Sunday. Prior to the attack, the army flew no dawn patrols, and Sundays were light duty days, making it an especially quiet time on base. When the attack came, most of the soldiers and sailors were either still asleep or eating their breakfast, completely unprepared to defend themselves, their bases, or their country.

at Ford Island, his white uniform was almost black, and he had to convince the marines patrolling the shore that he was not a Japanese invader. "I'm navy! I'm with the United States Navy! Don't shoot!" he shouted.[2]

Matthews spent the rest of the day helping the wounded and hauling damaged aircraft off the runways. Runways littered with wrecked aircraft would be useless if the enemy returned. The remaining men knew they had to be ready for a fight.

## MASS DESTRUCTION: AMERICAN LOSSES

Although the two waves of Japanese attacks lasted for less than two hours in total, the United States suffered massive losses of men and equipment: 2,403 people were killed, of whom 68 were civilians; 1,178 people were wounded; 188 aircraft were destroyed; and 21 ships were sunk, damaged, or destroyed, including battleships, cruisers, and destroyers.[4]

## THE ATTACK

Matthews was not the only one unprepared for a Japanese attack on the morning of December 7. The attack caught the entire US military off guard.

When Commander Logan C. Ramsey looked out from the Ford Island Command Center, he thought the low-flying aircraft he spotted was a careless US pilot. But when a black object dropped from the plane, Ramsey realized it was a bomb.

From the radio room, he telegraphed a hasty message, not even taking the time to put it in code. All bases and ships received this transmission: AIR RAID ON PEARL HARBOR. THIS IS NOT DRILL.[3] With this warning, the men did all they could to prepare for an attack, but for many the alert came too late.

## THE FATE OF THE USS *ARIZONA*

The USS *Arizona* was hit by several bombs, one of which penetrated the ship and detonated ammunition stores. The explosion ruptured the hull and gutted the front section of the ship. Turrets and other parts of the superstructure collapsed, and the ship sank, settling on the harbor floor.

Of the 1,512 men on board the *Arizona* at the time of the attack, 1,177 died.[5] This was nearly half of the total number of US soldiers and sailors lost that day. Many of the men aboard the *Arizona* died in the explosions or fires—but others drowned, trapped as the ship quickly sank. Matthews's friend Stafford was one of the many men killed that day.

At the time of the attack, the United States and Japan were not at war. However, leaders from both countries had been working in the background, preparing for the day that war would come. The Japanese had decided to attack on their terms instead of waiting for the Americans to strike the first blow.

## LIGHT LOSSES: THE JAPANESE STORY

The Japanese did not expect to attack Pearl Harbor without suffering any losses on their side. Indeed, they anticipated the destruction of up to three of their six aircraft carriers. Despite this, their actual losses included only 29 aircraft, 5 midget submarines, and 64 men killed.[6]

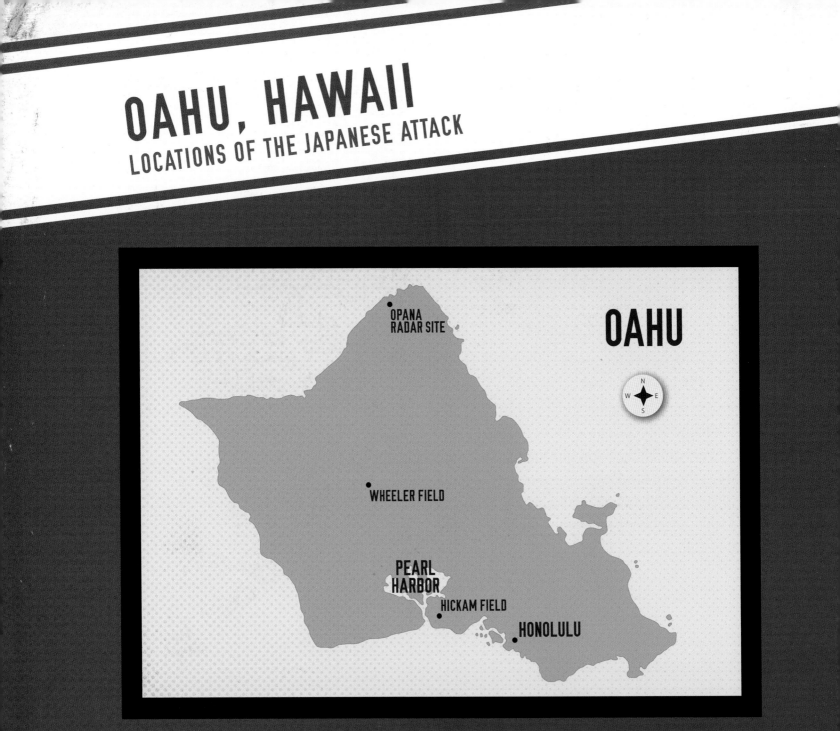

# OAHU, HAWAII
## LOCATIONS OF THE JAPANESE ATTACK

OAHU

OPANA RADAR SITE

WHEELER FIELD

PEARL HARBOR

HICKAM FIELD

HONOLULU

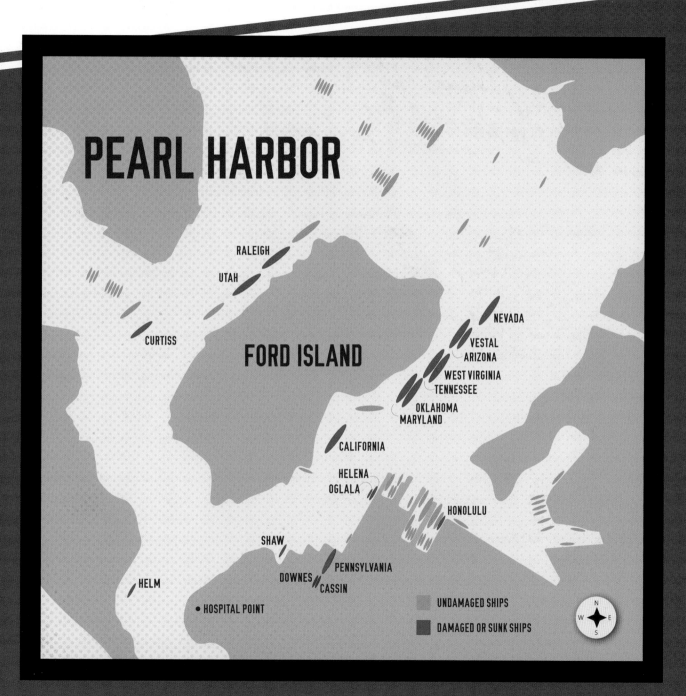

PEARL HARBOR

RALEIGH
UTAH
CURTISS

FORD ISLAND

NEVADA
VESTAL
ARIZONA
WEST VIRGINIA
TENNESSEE
OKLAHOMA
MARYLAND

CALIFORNIA

HELENA
OGLALA
HONOLULU

SHAW

HELM

DOWNES
CASSIN
PENNSYLVANIA

● HOSPITAL POINT

UNDAMAGED SHIPS

DAMAGED OR SUNK SHIPS

N
W E
S

# GLOBAL UNREST

When American Commodore Matthew Perry sailed into Tokyo Bay in 1853, he was not the first westerner to visit Japan. He was trying to reestablish a trade connection. More than 200 years earlier, the Japanese had had their fill of unfair trade agreements with the West. They were also unhappy with western missionaries trying to convert the Japanese to Catholicism. In 1639, Japan had expelled most foreigners, trading with only a few Chinese and Dutch ships each year.

Perry arrived in Tokyo Bay to deliver a letter asking for trade relations with Japan. The United States believed the Japanese had vast amounts of coal. And as ships moved from sail power to coal-fired steam, coal took on increasing importance to shipping and trade. Because Japan was between the United States and Chinese trade ports, Japan would be the ideal place to refuel and resupply.

When another fleet of ships returned to Japan a year after Perry's trip, Japanese leaders agreed to the demands made in the letter. Trade brought new ideas as well as material goods, and change rippled through Japan. In 1889, the government adopted its first constitution and established a legislature, the Imperial Diet. This change meant the Emperor no longer had full authority over the country. Japan also moved from being a strictly agricultural society to an industrial one, with machine-produced silk quickly making up 43 percent of Japan's exports.[1] Japanese leaders also industrialized their military, modernizing their ships and their weapons. The country soon became a Pacific power, defeating China in 1895 and Russia in 1905.

The Japanese had seen what happened to weak Asian countries: they became the colonies of stronger western countries. The Netherlands, for example, controlled the East Indies. As an island nation, Japan's own resources were limited. To become a world power safe from invasion or coercion by other nations, Japan needed a greater variety of resources. The country's leaders decided to get what they could by taking over areas that had the resources they needed. Japan's modernized military made this possible. So, in 1931, with the support of Emperor Hirohito,

## IMPERIALISM

A colony is a country controlled by a more powerful country. The stronger country sends in its own people to settle farms, ranches, and towns while also working to control the local government. Indochina, once a French colony, was made up of the modern countries of Vietnam, Cambodia, and Laos. The Dutch East Indies, once a colony of the Netherlands, are now known as the country of Indonesia. The United Kingdom controlled the colonies of Burma, Malaya, Singapore, and Brunei.

Japan invaded the Chinese province of Manchuria.

The time was ripe for such an expansion, as China was embroiled in civil war. China's Nationalists were led by Sun Yat-sen, who had been educated in the United States. The Nationalists were engaged in a bitter struggle against Mao Zedong's Communists. Japanese leaders believed expansion into Manchuria would give Japan access to steel, coal, and metals.

Japan thought invading China would result in an easy victory, but the Japanese military bogged down in this vast region. The fight cost Japan a great deal in terms of military resources and soldiers lost. When western powers, especially the United States, pressured Japan to get out of Manchuria, Japanese leaders refused. The Japanese believed they could not

Hirohito, *center*, was the emperor of Japan until his death in 1989.

afford to retreat—both because they had invested so much and because to do so would leave them looking weak.

The only way to achieve victory would be to devote still more resources to the cause, but Japan did not have these resources. To find what they needed, Japan's leaders would have to expand yet again. As Nazi Germany defeated France and the Netherlands in Europe in 1940, Japan began eyeing these countries' Asian colonies of Indochina and the Dutch East Indies. These colonies contained oil, tin, and rubber, all of which were essential wartime resources. So in July 1940, Japanese forces invaded Indochina. Then on September 27, Japan officially became an ally of Germany and Italy when it signed the Tripartite Pact.

## WESTERN ISOLATIONISM

Even while Japan was expanding, the United States appeared to be pulling back to focus on issues at home. Days after Germany's invasion of Poland on September 1, 1939, US president Franklin Delano Roosevelt told reporters, "There is no thought in any shape, manner, or form, of putting the nation, either in its defenses or in its internal economy, on a war basis."[2]

## HIROHITO'S ROLE

Emperor Hirohito, known among the Japanese as Tenno, was the ruler of Japan at the time of World War II. The Japanese military was a driving force behind the changes in that country. Some historians believe Hirohito was powerless to influence the military's decisions. Other historians note that although he might not have been able to bring the military's plans to a halt, he was not altogether innocent. "The decisions that led to the war in 1941 were made unanimously by the cabinet," says historian Richard B. Finn. "The emperor was fully informed about them, they were often made in his presence, he knew in advance of the plan to attack Hawaii, and he even made suggestions about how to carry it out."[3] Hirohito may not have had a great deal of power, but he had input in the coming battle.

Japanese soldiers make their way through wreckage during the invasion of China.

Roosevelt could not say anything else. He knew the American people well, and they wanted to avoid another war. Given the problems they believed World War I had caused, it was no surprise Americans did not want any part in another conflict. World War I had resulted in major losses of American manpower, with 116,500 men in the US military dying overseas.[4] In addition, World War I had led the US military to spend huge sums of money abroad rather than at home. Many Americans believed this loss of human resources and economic resources led directly to the Great Depression—a decade of high unemployment and failed businesses. For these reasons, many people in 1940 were driving around with stickers on their windshields that read "KEEP THE U.S. OUT OF WAR."[5]

Republican senator Gerald P. Nye of South Dakota went so far as to say US involvement in World War I was not a decision based on ethics. According to Nye, the United States had not gone to war to help allies or to help put down an evil regime. Instead, politicians, armament manufacturers, and bankers had tricked the United States into fighting.

As the number of countries fighting in both Europe and Asia grew in 1940, people worried the United States would once again

## PRO-CHINA

As the Japanese invasion of China turned into the Sino-Japanese War, an opinion poll published on October 24, 1937, showed 1 percent of Americans favored the Japanese while 59 percent favored the Chinese.[6] In part, this was because American missionaries in China told stories about the brutality of Japanese soldiers toward the Chinese people. In addition, rallies in the United States supported the Chinese while condemning the Japanese. Nevertheless, isolationist attitudes held strong, as 40 percent of Americans polled refused to take a side.[7]

# FRANKLIN D. ROOSEVELT

## 1882–1945

Franklin Delano Roosevelt was born on January 30, 1882, in Hyde Park, New York. He grew up wealthy and was educated by tutors. He respected his distant cousin, President Theodore Roosevelt—and, like his cousin, Franklin Roosevelt entered politics. In 1910, he was elected to the New York State Senate.

While on vacation in 1921, Roosevelt came down with polio. Although he survived, he never walked again under his own power. This is why many pictures of Roosevelt show him seated or using crutches. For a time, he believed this illness had ended his political career, but his wife and friends encouraged him to return to politics. Slowly, he regained his strength and learned to walk with crutches. He did not believe Americans would elect a man they considered weak.

Roosevelt was elected president in 1932. The United States was already in the depths of the Great Depression, with 13 million Americans unemployed.[8] During his first 100 days in office, Roosevelt helped pass laws to reform the country's banks. He told the American people about what he was doing in radio broadcasts called fireside chats.

As the Germans threatened Europe and the Japanese moved across Asia, Roosevelt turned his attention from jobs to global politics. He had to find a way to convince Americans it was again time to fight.

go to war—and that, once again, many young men would return home in coffins. Women's organizations, such as the National Legion of Mothers of America, worked to keep the United States out of the war.

Most people who spoke up against American involvement were not pacifists. Some of them, including radio personality Hedda Hopper, believed in "Fortress America," the idea that if the United States had a strong military, no country would risk an attack. They thought if war destroyed Europe, civilization would grow again from the United States. The key would be getting the military into this position of power without having to use it.

## GLOBAL CONFLICT

Roosevelt had won his third term as president by promising to keep the country out of any upcoming wars. This did not mean Roosevelt was an isolationist who wanted no involvement in other nations' affairs. He believed the United States had a responsibility to take part in world politics. And starting in the late 1930s, he spoke out against Nazi Germany because he saw the danger it posed to world peace and American interests.

The American people may have been committed to avoiding war, but Roosevelt saw the need to do more than speak out against Nazi Germany. American arms manufacturers stepped up production, and much of what they made was shipped to countries already fighting the Germans, particularly the United Kingdom.

The Germans invaded France in the spring of 1940, prompting Roosevelt to give the United Kingdom 50 US destroyers in exchange for military bases in the North Atlantic. This agreement, known as the Destroyers for Bases Agreement, was signed on September 2, 1940. The British needed these ships to continue the Battle of the Atlantic, which was an attempt to block all shipping to Germany while also breaking the German submarine blockade of all shipping to the United Kingdom.

As the fighting continued, the United Kingdom began running low on funds. Roosevelt started the Lend-Lease program, which enabled the United States to continue supplying its allies. Although the US military had not become involved in the fight, Roosevelt was moving the country closer to war.

## PUSHING JAPAN

In the 1930s, Roosevelt had seen Japan was expanding toward American interests. Guam, a US territory in the Pacific Ocean, served as a stopping point for US ships and aircraft. And the Philippines, an island nation in Southeast Asia, was a US trade partner and ally. Roosevelt wanted to keep these vital locations safe from Japan. Because of the isolationist feelings of so many Americans, Roosevelt was not willing to commit to war against Japan—but he could pressure Japan in other ways.

### LEND-LEASE

Despite most Americans' reluctance to enter the war, Roosevelt was determined to provide US allies with the materials they needed to fight. The Lend-Lease Act, signed in March 1941, allowed the United States to transfer weapons or other materials to any ally in need if their defense was vital to the United States. Because many war-torn countries were short of money, Lend-Lease stipulated these countries would not have to pay for the materials until after the war. The Lend-Lease program enabled the United States to aid the United Kingdom and China, among others.

Japan needed a large amount of steel and fuel for its military actions in China and purchased many of these supplies from the United States. Therefore, the US government halted the export of oil and steel to Japan in October 1940. The move immediately brought protests from Japanese leaders, who accused the United States of "economic strangulation."[9] When the Japanese leaders made this protest, American negotiators asked for even more concessions, demanding Japan break off its alliance with Germany and Italy and retreat from its holdings in China and Southeast Asia.

The Japanese had no intention of doing any of these things because Japanese leaders did not want other nations to see them as weak. Instead, their negotiators demanded the United States break off all ties with the Chinese Nationalists, who were fighting against the Japanese in China. They also demanded the Americans begin selling steel and oil to Japan again.

As Japanese forces moved farther into Southeast Asia, the US government decided to send a stronger message. The US Army and Navy may not have been ready to fight, but the military could make it look as if they were. Therefore, the navy moved the Pacific Fleet from its harbor in California to Pearl Harbor, Hawaii, as if poised and waiting to move on Japan.

Japanese officials celebrated with their German and Italian counterparts after signing the Tripartite Pact in 1940.

Japanese aircraft carriers *Zuikaku, foreground,* and *Kaga, background,* travel toward Hawaii in November 1941.

# JAPAN'S PLAN

The Japanese military had planned for a confrontation with the US Navy for decades. In the original plan, portions of the Japanese navy would simultaneously attack several places south of Japan while the main body of the fleet remained in Japanese waters. The Japanese knew the US Navy would head toward Japan in order to retaliate, so Japan worked to make sure the US Navy would never reach Japan. Somewhere east of Japan's home islands, the Japanese navy would attack and destroy the US fleet bit by bit, battle by battle.

The location of this planned confrontation changed as the Japanese navy grew. Larger, faster ships meant battles could be fought farther from Japan itself. By 1938, Japan planned to make its stand near the Mariana Islands, east of the Philippines.

The US Navy developed its own plan, known as Plan Orange. The US Navy would indeed proceed toward Japan, but Plan

Orange included taking a variety of Japanese-held islands along the way before encountering and destroying the Japanese navy.

Both the Japanese and American plans included aircraft carriers, a type of ship developed after World War I. These huge ships were so new that military strategists still did not know how to effectively incorporate carriers into battle plans. Before the bombing of Pearl Harbor, one or two aircraft carriers would accompany a division of ships, and the limited number of aircraft available would be used as scout planes or to form a small raiding party. The Japanese were about to change this way of thinking forever.

## AIRCRAFT CARRIERS

The first aircraft carrier to be built "from the keel up," rather than being converted from an existing ship, was the Japanese ship *Hōshō*, commissioned in December 1922. This flat-topped ship looked very different from other ships in the Imperial Japanese Navy because, when the smokestacks were collapsed for aircraft takeoff, the upper part of the ship was all flight deck. This runway sat atop the rest of the ship, including the hangar bays belowdecks where the ship carried 21 aircraft.[1]

Building a ship from the keel takes time. One of the quickest ways to add a carrier to a navy or convoy was to convert another ship already in use or build the carrier on the keel of a ship under construction. The second Japanese aircraft carrier, the *Akagi*, had originally been a battle cruiser. In its role as a carrier, the *Akagi* transported 60 aircraft.[2]

The *Zuikaku* and *Shokaku*, both built from the keel, each transported a maximum of 84 aircraft.[3]

The Japanese aircraft carrier *Hiryu*, which took part in the Pearl Harbor attack, was destroyed by American fighter planes in 1942.

## FLOATING AIRFIELDS

At the beginning of World War II, military strategists began using navies to create mobile fighting forces beyond the limits of land. Previously, a fleet of ships could approach lands held by an enemy or move a fighting force around mountainous or boggy areas that were otherwise impassable. But destinations were limited to areas where the fighting force could actually get off the ships, making access to a harbor essential.

Aircraft carriers changed this because they operate as mobile airfields. Unlike ground troops, aircraft do not need a harbor in order to disembark. Therefore, carriers extended the reach of the aircraft and pilots, providing mobile landing and fueling stations. Just as important, aircraft carriers also extended the reach of the military that wielded them. Access to a harbor was no longer essential for military success. A fleet organized around aircraft carriers presented a very different fighting force than had been seen in the past. With a carrier to provide a landing strip, planes could attack targets that potential enemies would have previously believed were secure.

American military advisers expected the Japanese to go after US targets in Asia or the western Pacific, such as the Philippines. This was how the Japanese had operated in the past—by keeping the bulk of their navy safely in home waters while using a smaller force to attack nearby targets.

## JAPANESE AIRCRAFT

Japanese World War II aircraft, especially the Mitsubishi fighter planes that Americans called Zeroes, quickly earned a reputation for excellence because of their high speed and maneuverability. To achieve this, engineers reduced the plane's weight by eliminating everything they could, including armor. They also chose not to use self-sealing fuel tanks, which, because of layers of rubber, were heavier than other fuel tanks. Therefore, enemy bullets could easily puncture the skin of the aircraft and the fuel tank. Unable to seal a leak, a damaged tank would spill highly flammable fuel.

A Zero plane takes off from a Japanese aircraft carrier on the morning of the Pearl Harbor attack.

However, the Japanese navy realized it could now set its sights on targets thousands of miles from home thanks to its new aircraft carriers. Admiral Isoroku Yamamoto, the commander in chief of Japan's fleet, decided to use the Japanese carriers as part of a new "defensive-reactive" strategy. Japanese carriers would form part of a mobile strike force known as the First Air Fleet, composed of Japanese carriers and their various escort ships. This arrangement put all eight of Japan's carriers and approximately 400 aircraft under one commander, creating a mobile strike force unlike anything in history.[4] The Japanese navy could now strike farther from their homeland than ever before—and in January 1941, Yamamoto came up with the idea to use this force to attack the US Navy in Pearl Harbor.

Initially, Japan's Navy General Staff opposed this plan, fearing they would fail to defeat the Americans and that their own navy would be destroyed in the process. Yamamoto led a series of military exercises that convinced the others his plan would work—and it would work largely because of Japan's two new aircraft carriers, the *Zuikaku* and the *Shokaku*. Once Yamamoto had the backing of the Navy General Staff and trained pilots, the First Air Fleet was poised to sweep the seas. But first, the fleet had to reach Hawaii unnoticed.

Carriers gave navies the ability to fight far from home, but they also created a new level of vulnerability. These huge ships had some guns, but they were not heavily armed or armored. And compared with the rest of the fleet, carriers were slow moving. This meant carriers were hard to defend and put the rest of the fleet at risk. To counteract this problem, a fleet relying on carriers had to strike first and strike fast in order to take out the enemy's carriers and take their planes out of the battle. The force that destroyed the enemy's carriers first would, over time, emerge the winner.

Yamamoto saw this immediate victory as essential. He believed Japan would lose a drawn-out war against the United States. Therefore, the only hope for victory was to hit the Americans with a devastating initial strike. By inflicting great damage in the first attack, Yamamoto expected American morale to be so

# ISOROKU YAMAMOTO

## 1884–1943

Admiral Isoroku Yamamoto, the commander in chief of Japan's combined fleet and mastermind behind the bombing of Pearl Harbor, graduated from the Japanese Naval Academy in 1904. After being wounded during the Russo-Japanese War, he returned to school and attended the Japanese navy's staff college before studying at Harvard University in the United States. From 1925 to 1928, he served as a naval expert at Japan's embassy in Washington, DC.

Yamamoto was a well-educated soldier, but he also knew the people of the United States. He opposed a Japanese alliance with Germany because he realized this would push Japan into war with the United States. When it became obvious that battle was coming soon, he was loyal to Japan and planned for a strike that would defeat the US Navy.

He modeled his plan after the German blitzkrieg, or "lightning war," in Europe. The goal was to hit the enemy hard and overwhelm them. Yamamoto believed an attack that hit the United States hard enough would require years of recovery before the Americans could fully engage in the war—and by that time, Japan would have consolidated its hold throughout Asia.

low the US government would negotiate a settlement rather than get involved in a war.

This sweeping victory would be possible only if the Japanese reached their destination undetected. To do so, they had to keep their movements secret from the US military. The plan to accomplish this feat started with the Japanese radio operators.

## RADIO OPERATORS

The Japanese had already learned the Americans and the British were highly skilled at intercepting radio signals. Early in the summer of 1941, when Japan moved to occupy French military facilities in Indochina, a Japanese carrier's radio transmissions had been intercepted by the British and were used to locate the ships. The Japanese knew that even if the British and Americans could not decode a message, they could still use it to locate a fleet.

For the planned attack on Pearl Harbor to work, surprise was essential. Therefore, the Japanese planned to use radio signals to deceive the US military about the location of Japan's fleet. By setting up an elaborate trick, Japan hoped to convince the United States the Japanese fleet was in one place when it was actually someplace completely different. On November 15, 1941, new call signs were assigned to the various ships. The Japanese issued new call signs on a regular basis, so this alone would not alert the United States that something was in the works.

Each Japanese radio operator had a recognizable fist, or unique way he tapped out a message in Morse code. Other radio operators, whether in the Japanese navy or among the US radiomen listening in, could recognize the fist of each

## DEFENSIVE INFORMATION PATROL

On December 1, 1941, the Japanese replaced their call signs, which caught the attention of US military advisers. Although the Japanese regularly replaced call signs, this was not a scheduled replacement. US advisers believed the Japanese must be getting ready for something big. They assumed it would be an attack on the Philippines or elsewhere in the western Pacific.

To find out where Japan would strike, Roosevelt ordered three small ships to wait along the expected route of the Japanese navy. Each ship would be under the command of one US officer and have the smallest crew possible. Roosevelt issued the order on December 1, but only one ship was in position by December 5—too late to see the Japanese fleet that had already passed.

Japanese operator and knew which ship he worked on. By hearing different fists, US radiomen could determine where Japanese operators—and Japanese ships—were located.

Because of this fact, the Japanese radiomen who normally worked aboard ships were transferred to three separate naval bases on the Japanese home islands. When US listening posts heard a fist they recognized, they would believe the Japanese radio operator's ship was located in the direction from which the signal came. And because each signal would come from the direction of that ship's home harbor, the Americans would assume the ships were inactive.

Once the Japanese operators were at the bases, they began sending a series of fake messages. The messages were carefully timed to fit the pattern of normal radio traffic. To keep from confusing Japanese radiomen who would also hear the messages, the false messages were sent in dummy groups, or fake codes

British soldiers learn how to operate radios for the Royal Air Force.

not normally used by the Japanese. This constant traffic would convince American listening stations they were hearing normal chatter. The Americans would not realize these operators were now sending messages from land-based locations while the ships secretly traveled to a meet-up point in Japan's Inland Sea.

## ONGOING NEGOTIATIONS

While both the Japanese and the Americans made plans for war, they also negotiated. The United States had halted all trade with Japan, and the island nation was suffering through serious shortages. The Japanese would negotiate as long as there was a chance of getting the material goods they needed.

Every request for trade by the Japanese was met by the same US demand: pull out of China. Because Japan had no intention of leaving China, further negotiations were pointless. Even so, Yamamoto needed his diplomats in place until the last moment. Their final job was one of honor—to deliver one last message to the Americans, breaking off diplomatic relations.

## TOTAL SILENCE

After the Japanese fleet departed from the Inland Sea for Pearl Harbor on November 26, 1941, the ships in the fleet went into complete radio silence. False

### JAPANESE HONOR

Under the Japanese code of honor, attacking another country while still negotiating with them would be inappropriate. As much as the Japanese military wanted to wipe out the US Navy, they wanted to do so with honor. Right before the attack, the Japanese embassy was to deliver a message breaking off all relations with the US government. However, a clerical error delayed the decryption and delivery of the message until after the attack on Pearl Harbor had begun.

transmissions would not be enough to cover their true location. If the ships themselves sent radio signals that no longer lined up with Japanese waters, and instead came from locations where no Japanese ships were supposed to be, their cover would be blown.

To ensure that an anxious captain or operator could not send a message, radio transmitters were locked up or disabled. Slips of paper were inserted between the contacts of transmitting keys on the telegraphs. Fuses and parts of the circuits were removed. The communications officer of the battleship *Hiei* went so far as to put the transmitter in a box that he kept beneath his head while he slept.

## PEARL HARBOR PREPARATION

An attack on Pearl Harbor would require overcoming two logistical difficulties: the mountainous terrain surrounding the bay, and the shallow bay itself. The average depth of the bay was only 45 feet (14 m), and most aerial torpedoes needed depths of at least 100 feet (30 m) to avoid striking the ocean bottom when dropped. To solve this problem, Commander Minoru Genda, a Japanese pilot, added wooden tail fins to the torpedoes. This addition reduced the torpedoes' speed on entry and also limited the depth to which they would descend after striking the water.

Throughout the summer of 1941, Japanese pilots practiced in Kagoshima Bay. They flew low over the northern ridges and down through a twisting valley in a landscape that resembled Pearl Harbor. Innovation and practice prepared this force to take on the US Navy in Pearl Harbor.

## NO PATROLS

The original plan for the attack also included sending out reconnaissance planes from the carriers to scout ahead. This would assure the Japanese the American ships were in their expected locations and that there was no change in activity.

When the time came to send out these patrols, Admiral Chūichi Nagumo, commander of the task force, decided it was too risky for two reasons. First of all, there was concern that American planes from Midway Atoll or Alaska's Aleutian Islands might spot the distinctly marked Japanese aircraft. The other concern was that if one of the Japanese pilots got lost, he would ask for a navigational beacon or radio directions. This, of course, would compromise the radio silence, meaning US posts might overhear the signal and realize Japanese forces were in the area. Instead of flying patrols, the Japanese kept six aircraft on deck for emergencies and scouted only on the day of the attack, maintaining secrecy until the last possible moment.

Admiral Nagumo committed suicide in 1944 after being defeated in the Battle of Saipan.

# LIMITED INTELLIGENCE

Whether the Japanese would be able to sneak up on Pearl Harbor depended not only on their plan, but also on the abilities and limitations of the US military. First and foremost among these limitations was the Americans' inability to understand the Japanese naval code. Called the JN-25 Fleet Operational Code, the Japanese navy used this extremely complicated code to send approximately 70 percent of its messages.[1] Because US intelligence had been unable to break the code, most messages sent by the Japanese navy were unreadable by US code breakers—in large part because writing and decoding messages required several code books the Americans did not have.

Without these code books, the US military could decode only 30 percent of the messages sent by the Japanese navy.[2] But this was not the only problem the Americans faced when dealing with Japanese messages.

## ACCESS BLOCKED

The Japanese government blocked access to many common sources of information, censoring all Japanese newspapers and limiting ship and aircraft traffic where people might observe the Japanese military. Without these sources, American knowledge of Japanese ship locations was based solely on radio signals. A radio signal enabled the Americans to find the direction from which the message had been sent—and therefore, the ship that had sent it. Intelligence based on a single source can be easily exploited, however, and that is exactly what the Japanese did. With the addition of newspaper reports or eyewitness sightings, the United States might not have been fooled.

## NEED TO KNOW

Although the United States had not broken the Japanese naval code, American cryptographers had broken the code used by Japanese diplomats. This gave the United States access to all messages between the Japanese Foreign Secretary and Japan's ambassadors in Washington, DC. Instructions about negotiations and relations could be intercepted and decoded, and the information was put to use by the US government and military.

The problem was that only a small group of people, known as Ultras, were allowed to read these diplomatic messages. The Ultras included President Roosevelt; George Marshall, the army chief of staff; Harold Rainsford Stark, the chief of naval operations; the secretary of state; the secretary of war; and the secretary of the navy.

Every person who saw a decoded message was a potential leak—someone who might intentionally or accidentally reveal information to an enemy spy. Radioing a decoded message was risky because the signal could be intercepted just as US listening stations had intercepted the original Japanese message. The Ultras did not want anyone else to know that even one Japanese code had been broken, because if this information got out, the Japanese would replace the code and the United States would have access to much less information. The decoded messages could not be trusted to a radio message, telegraph, or scrambled phone call. Instead, copies of the messages were placed in locked pouches and transported by two couriers. After each Ultra had read the message, he gave it back to the waiting courier. The courier then returned the message to the appropriate department for his branch of the service, and all but one file copy was destroyed.

## COMMUNICATION BREAKDOWN

This process limited the amount of time the Ultras had with the information and may have limited their ability to fully consider the implications of what they read. Because they were not allowed to discuss the information, they were not entirely certain who had access to it and who did not. Some men, including Admiral Husband Kimmel and Lieutenant General Walter Campbell Short, made important military decisions without information their superiors sometimes assumed they had.

On November 22, Admiral Kimmel halted all long-distance patrol flights by navy aircraft without telling either

## GATHERING INFORMATION

The US military had three ways to gather information on the Japanese: cryptanalysis, radio direction finding, and traffic analysis. Cryptanalysis is a military term for code breaking. Radio direction finding is a means of locating the radio transmitter that sent a message. With readings from three different listening stations, an analyst can track the direction from which each station received the message. The spot where the lines cross is the location of the transmitter. Traffic analysis is the study of radio traffic. Call signs are codes that identify either the radio operator or the transmitter. Traffic analysts look at the amount of traffic and number of messages being sent, as well as which call sign is sending messages to which other call sign.

Lieutenant General Short or Admiral Stark. Kimmel made this decision because he had so few planes and men that he believed he could not adequately patrol the area. If his patrols found anything, it would be due to simple luck. Given this limited chance of success, Kimmel did not think it was worth the risk of either navy equipment or lives. By canceling patrol flights, he could focus navy manpower and resources on better training the inexperienced pilots and crews currently staffing his planes.

General Short of the army was not flying patrols either. He was worried about sabotage. To keep his aircraft safe, he ordered the planes near Pearl Harbor to be grouped close together on the runways outside of the hangars. Clustering the aircraft in the open reduced the number of people required to guard them. However, the planes were not combat ready and could not be made ready in less than four hours.

On November 27, a message went out from Admiral Stark to General Short. In part, the communication read:

> *Negotiations with Japan appear to be terminated to all practical purposes with only the barest possibilities that the Japanese Government might come back and offer to continue. Japanese future action unpredictable but hostile action possible at any moment. . . . [You] are directed to undertake such reconnaissance and other measures as you deem necessary but these measures should be carried out so as not, repeat not, to alarm civil population or disclose intent.[3]*

Because the communication did not clearly state that an air attack was imminent or that Short should be on the lookout for enemy forces, he continued focusing on keeping his planes safe from sabotage. This was the hostile action he had been looking for before receiving the message, and nothing in the message changed his focus. Because Marshall and Stark, both Ultras, did not object, Short assumed his plans met with their approval. He also relied on Kimmel's nonexistent reconnaissance patrols to provide information about approaching enemies. Meanwhile, Kimmel had confidence in the defense capabilities of Short's noncombat ready aircraft. If Short or Kimmel had had more information, they might have made better decisions.

## THREAT UNEXPECTED

Perhaps the United States would not have been so easy to surprise if military advisers had considered such an attack possible. In hearings following the bombing of Pearl Harbor, General Marshall testified that although the greatest threat to Pearl Harbor would come from carrier-based aircraft, he in no way expected an attack of that kind.

Admiral Kimmel's testimony was even more pointed when he stated that he did not think the Japanese could pull off an attack of this scale so far from home. These assumptions about what the Japanese could and could not do would cost the United States dearly.

## TOO LITTLE, TOO LATE

The US military in Pearl Harbor was not actively looking for enemy aircraft, and even when someone spotted them, no one realized what they were. From 4:00 a.m. until 7:00 a.m. on the morning of December 7, search radar operators at the Opana Radar Site north of Honolulu manned their stations as part of a training operation. Because their transportation was late arriving, they stayed at the oscilloscopes so the newest member of the team could gain more experience. At 7:02 a.m., they spotted a "large radar return."[4] The signal indicated a large number of aircraft 135 miles (217 km) away headed in their direction.[5]

General Short faced legal charges for his role in allowing the Pearl Harbor attack

American planes are parked outside at an air station near Pearl Harbor.

The radar operator contacted the pursuit officer on duty at the Information Center to report the sighting. The pursuit officer's job was to give instructions to US aircraft being sent after the enemy. On December 7, this job had been assigned to Lieutenant Kermit Tyler, who was new at his post. Tyler knew a flight of B-17s from California was due in Hawaii shortly, and he assumed the traffic was these US planes. But because this information was "need to know," he could not explain the situation to the operators. "Don't worry about it," said Tyler.[6] In only 35 minutes, they would realize just how worried they should have been.

## SLOW AND SLOWEST

Although analysts could not decrypt most of the Japanese navy's messages, they had a large number of diplomatic messages to decrypt. Between this large volume of coded messages and the limited number of code breakers, cryptanalysis was a painfully slow process. An important military message might sit in line for hours behind numerous messages about diplomatic dinners and parties before anyone realized it was there.

A Japanese midget submarine runs aground on the eastern shore of Oahu.

# SUBMARINES

Even before the operator at the Opana Radar Site spotted a suspicious blip on his scope, the Japanese had already surrounded the Hawaiian Islands. By December 6, as many as 25 submarines lay hidden below the surface of the sea.[1] Five of them transported a whole new type of ship: the Japanese midget submarine.[2]

The Japanese transport submarines brought the midget submarines within a few miles of Pearl Harbor and then off-loaded them. Pearl Harbor would be their first battle, and the US Navy their first target. Their task was to sneak into the harbor undetected and wait for the aerial attack to begin. Once the Japanese aircraft arrived, these subs would launch their torpedoes, enabling the Japanese fleet to attack the mighty American navy not only from the air but also from beneath the sea.

## THE PLAN

At only 80 feet (24 m) long, each two-man midget submarine was a quarter of the length of its transport sub. Each midget sub was powered by an electric motor that propelled it forward at 19 knots, or nearly 22 miles per hour (35 kmh), making it almost twice as fast as most of the larger submarines in use.[3] Each midget sub was equipped with two torpedoes that could be launched before the vessel made its escape. In contrast, later Japanese subs such as the Kaiten were designed to ram their targets, essentially making them suicide machines.

To get into position for the attack at Pearl Harbor, the midget subs had to get past the antitorpedo net, which was a massive construction of interlocking loops of steel cable that lurked beneath the water and guarded the harbor's entrance. To get past the net, each sub was equipped with two special pieces of equipment. First, a cutter sliced through the net. Then a cable, attached to a pulley, guided the cut net up and over the sub, allowing the craft to pass beneath it without catching.

## THE KAITEN

In late 1944, the Japanese developed the Kaiten-class miniature submarine, which was also called a manned torpedo. Unlike earlier Japanese minisubs, this was not a ship to be used and reused. The pilot of this suicide sub was locked into a central compartment. Once inside, the pilot guided his ship into a target and blew himself up. The Japanese navy stated that these ships sunk two American ships, including the USS *Underhill*.

The control room of each midget submarine contained many instruments, including a

## EXECUTING THE PLAN

Although the midget subs launched as planned, their entrance into the harbor did not go entirely undetected. At approximately 3:30 a.m., the US minesweeper *Condor* spotted something in the water—a periscope where no submarine was supposed to be. The *Condor* sent a message to the USS *Ward*, alerting the destroyer to a submarine in the area.

## STILL NO ALARM

When the USS *Ward* sank the first midget submarine, the *Ward*'s commander sent out a message: "We have dropped depth charges upon sub operating in defensive sea area." He wanted to make certain that his message was understood. This was more than a suspected sighting because he had sunk an actual submarine. He sent a second message: "We have attacked, fired upon, and dropped depth charges upon submarine operating in defensive sea area."[4] Despite his efforts, no alarm was sounded. Admiral Kimmel later said that because there had been so many false submarine sightings, he did not want to take any action before making certain a sub had actually been seen.

At 6:45 a.m., more than an hour before the aerial attack began, the *Ward* fired on the midget submarine that had been spotted by the *Condor*. Although the destroyer's first shot missed entirely, the second struck the submarine at the waterline, causing the submarine to roll and then sink. To make sure the submarine was destroyed, the *Ward* dropped depth charges. As these charges sank, water pressure caused them to explode. The first midget submarine sank without firing either torpedo.

After the aerial attack began, another midget submarine ran aground on a reef on the east side of Oahu. This sub was spotted by a lookout on the destroyer USS *Helm*. The *Helm* fired and missed, giving the

The wreckage of a midget submarine was brought ashore after the attack.

submarine time to free itself from the reef and submerge. Before it could escape, the submarine snagged a second time and began to sink, drowning one crewman. The captain fought his way out of the sinking submarine and struggled ashore, where he was captured and became the United States' first prisoner of World War II. This submarine did not make it into the harbor, and, again, neither torpedo was fired.

The third submarine used its cutter and cable to enter Pearl Harbor, where it remained hidden until the aerial attack began. It managed to fire its torpedoes, but they both missed their targets and a US ship spotted the submarine. The US ship sent out a signal, and the destroyer *Monaghan* attacked, bearing down on the submarine at maximum speed while firing its guns. The destroyer rammed the smaller craft and then dropped a series of depth charges, eliminating the submarine.

No one knew what happened to the fourth submarine until 1960, when it was found south of the harbor. It still contained both torpedoes.

## WAR BENEATH THE WAVES

Unlike their German allies, the Japanese rarely used submarines against commercial shipping. Instead, the Japanese used their submarines against military targets. This included land-based targets such as Ellwood Oilfield and Fort Stevens, but more often the targets were military ships. Compared with merchant ships, the heavily armored military ships cruised at faster speeds and maneuvered more quickly, making them harder to hit.

The slow-moving Japanese subs became targets themselves when, in the summer of 1942, the Allies perfected radar that could detect ships running at night with no lights. This was a problem for the Japanese because their diesel submarines had to run on the surface for several hours every night to recharge their batteries.

If the war had lasted longer, the Japanese might have had success with the Sentoku submarine. The brainchild of Admiral Yamamoto, each of these subs was longer than a football field and capable of launching up to three airplanes at inland targets. Only three Sentoku subs had been built by the end of the war, and two were on their first mission when Japan surrendered.

In 1960, American sailors recovered a midget submarine that had been missing for

The fate of the fifth sub remained a mystery until 2002, when a Japanese midget submarine was found south of Pearl Harbor. This submarine was not sunk by the US Navy but by its own crew, who had been instructed to keep this secret weapon out of enemy hands. They set off a scuttling charge, tearing their own ship into three pieces.

Investigators who examined the wreckage discovered both torpedoes had been fired. They conducted a document search, reading all of the historical papers they could find about Pearl Harbor, and found a report that Admiral Chester Nimitz made to Congress stating the navy had found a dud torpedo. The torpedo was too large to have come from an aircraft but identical to those used by the midget submarines. Investigators also found a photograph of the day of the bombing that shows rooster tails, or plumes of water, heading toward two ships, the *West Virginia* and the *Oklahoma*. The investigators could not determine whether one of these torpedoes hit because of conflicting eyewitness accounts.

## TYPE 97

Before leaving the mother submarine, each midget submarine was armed with two Type 97 torpedoes. The 18-inch (46 cm) torpedoes were slipped into doorless, external torpedo tubes and launched by compressed air. Once launched, the torpedo sped through the water at 50 miles per hour (80 kmh) and could run at this speed for up to three miles (4.8 km).[5]

Even if one of these torpedoes did hit, the midget submarines proved far less effective than the Japanese had hoped. Part of the problem came from the fact that these small ships could not outmaneuver warships, and they sometimes ran aground. Midget submarines maneuvered poorly because their undersized

Of the ten men who operated midget submarines during the attack, Kazuo Sakamaki, seen here in 1961, was the only one to survive.

rudders kept them from turning quickly, making them hard to steer. The Japanese constantly improved their ship designs, and this rudder was changed immediately after the attack on Pearl Harbor. The Japanese submarines may have failed to do any significant damage, but the same cannot be said for the aircraft they were sent to support.

Japanese planes prepare to take off on the morning of the Pearl Harbor attack.

# THE FIRST WAVE OF AIRCRAFT

Admiral Stark had warned General Short about hostile actions. An American ship had sunk a midget submarine. Despite these warnings, the Americans were completely unprepared for what was to come.

## 6:10 A.M.

Thirty-five minutes before the USS *Ward* fired on the Japanese midget submarine, the carriers in the Japanese fleet turned into the wind in preparation for their planes taking off. The aircraft that made up the first wave of the Japanese attack roared down the flight decks and took off, approximately 200 miles (320 km) north of Hawaii.[1] The time to take out the US Navy had come.

## 7:40 A.M.

The Japanese planes—49 high-altitude bombers, 51 dive bombers, 40 torpedo planes, and 43 fighters—reached the northernmost point of the island of Oahu.[2] Most of the aircraft were painted a light gray with a vague hint of green, but Commander Mitsuo Fuchida's plane had a vibrant red tail to make it easy for his men to identify him.

Fuchida did not see any abnormal activity around the island, so he fired off a signal flare. This flare told his men they had arrived undetected and alerted the torpedo planes to attack first. The planes flew together for several more minutes before breaking into groups, each with a specific target.

## 7:55 A.M.

Dive bombers swooped down low and dropped their bombs on Wheeler Field north of the harbor and Hickam Field near the harbor's mouth. The Japanese targeted the airfields to eliminate as many aircraft as possible, hoping to stop a counterattack. Using incendiary bombs to burn equipment, the Japanese did heavy damage to the American aircraft that were clearly visible sitting on the runways. General

### TORA! TORA! TORA!

"Tora! Tora! Tora!" was a message radioed from Mitsuo Fuchida's plane to Admiral Nagumo.[3] Fuchida had fired a flare, which signaled to the other Japanese pilots they had arrived unnoticed. Back at the fleet, however, Admiral Nagumo would be unable to see this signal. To keep his commander informed, Fuchida radioed the admiral letting him know their arrival was a surprise and the attack was about to begin.

In Japanese, *tora* means "tiger." However, the word was used to mean "lightning attack." With the attack under way, radio silence could now be broken.

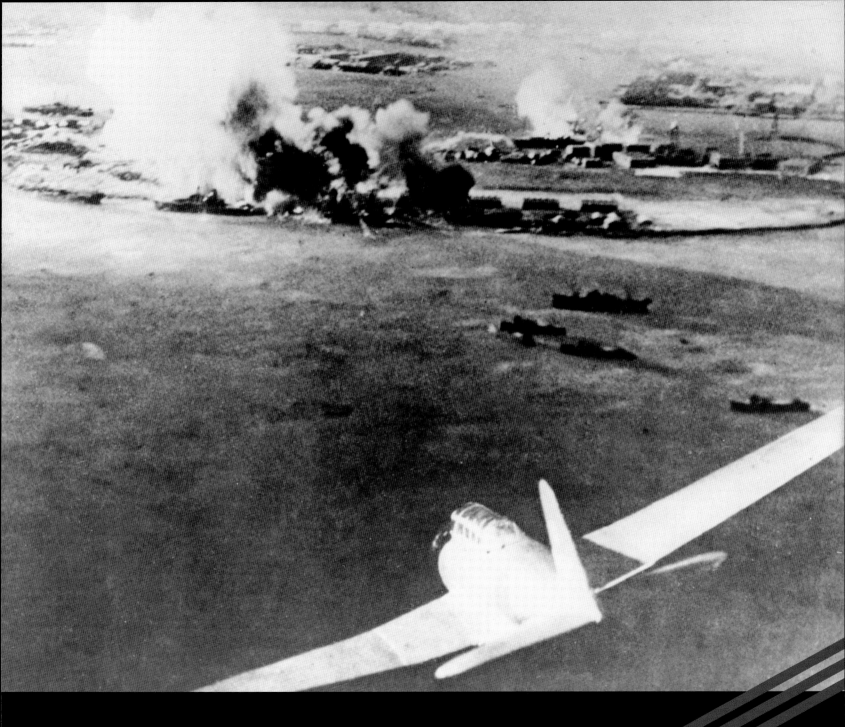

A Japanese bomber flies above Pearl Harbor as American ships burn below.

Short had left the aircraft on the runways so they could be easily guarded against sabotage; now they made easy targets.

Another group of aircraft launched torpedoes into the docks along Ford Island in the middle of the harbor. This area normally held the US aircraft carriers, but all three carriers were out of the port that day. This was bad news for the Japanese, as destroying the American aircraft carriers had been one of the attack's primary goals.

Then came the most destructive part of the attack, as 24 torpedo planes flying in groups of three launched their payloads into Battleship Row.[4] Takeo Yoshikawa, a Japanese spy living in Hawaii, had told the Japanese where various ships were docked.

At this early hour, many of the American sailors were belowdecks, unable to hear the aircraft and unaware of their presence until the torpedoes hit. Striking at or below the waterline, the torpedoes punctured the ships' hulls, causing massive flooding. The *California*, the fleet's flagship, lay at anchor nearest the harbor entrance. Two torpedoes struck the ship. It sank, coming to rest on the harbor floor. At least five torpedoes hit the *Oklahoma* and tore open the left side of the ship. As it flooded with water, the ship capsized. At least six torpedoes struck the *West Virginia*, breaching its hull midship and damaging the rudder.

## KIMMEL WATCHES

When the attack on Pearl Harbor began, Admiral Kimmel was at home, ten minutes from headquarters. He watched the first part of the attack from his neighbor's garden. Reaching headquarters just as the torpedo strike ended, he watched the remainder of the attack through a window. A spent round crashed through the glass, hitting Kimmel in the chest and leaving a welt.

# TAKEO YOSHIKAWA

## 1914–1993

The son of a policeman, Takeo Yoshikawa graduated with honors from the Imperial Japanese Naval College. He served on a battleship and trained with both aircraft and submarines, but illness forced him to retire while he was still a young man.

After the navy offered him a job in intelligence, Yoshikawa studied English for four years and learned everything he could about the US Navy and its bases in the Pacific. Once he had finished these studies, he was posted in Honolulu, where he posed as a diplomat named Tadashi Morimura.

In Hawaii, he quickly got to know the bases on Oahu and focused his attention on Pearl Harbor, the anchorage for the US Navy Pacific Fleet. Yoshikawa observed the fleet from the second-story window of a local teahouse and also from the nearby sugar cane fields. All information he gathered was coded and telegraphed to his superiors in Japan.

One of the messages he sent his superiors divided the waters of Pearl Harbor into five zones and detailed which ships would be berthed where. Although the United States decoded this message, only the Ultras knew the Japanese had this information.

Like the *California*, the *West Virginia* sank, settling on the harbor floor. The *Nevada* got off lightly with only one torpedo strike. The ship managed to cast off and head toward the harbor entrance, but the destruction at Battleship Row was not over.

## PLANE SPOTTING

The Japanese attacked Pearl Harbor using several types of aircraft.

High-altitude bombers flew at high altitudes to drop large bombs. These bombs did a great deal of damage but were not precise because they were dropped from thousands of feet. High-altitude bombers were often used against land-based targets.

Dive bombers would aim directly at the target, dive down, drop the bomb, and then pull up and away. The bombs they dropped were smaller, but dive-bombing was more accurate than high-altitude bombing.

Torpedo planes carried torpedoes for use against ships. When they dropped a torpedo into the water, a propeller would drive the torpedo forward.

Fighter planes were armed with guns. They did less damage to ground targets but were effective against other planes.

## 8:10 A.M.

Ten minutes after the first torpedoes dropped, a mass of Japanese bombers passed two miles (3.2 km) overhead. Each of these high-altitude bombers carried an 1,800-pound (800 kg) bomb adapted from a 16-inch (41 cm) battleship shell.[5] These bombers were not as effective as the torpedoes. While the heavy bombs generally damaged the superstructure of the ship, they failed to puncture the armor, so they did not cause flooding belowdecks.

The exception to this was the *Arizona*, the ship Martin Matthews watched sink. A heavy bomb hit led to a fire, which breached the main ammunition storage area and turned the ship into a mass of wreckage that burned for two days.

Sailors on the dock could only watch as several ships burned.

## 8:17 A.M.

A lookout on the USS *Helm* spotted the Japanese midget submarine that had run aground on the reef.

## 8:39 A.M.

The *Monaghan* fired on and rammed another midget submarine.

## SINKING SHIPS

If there is enough time, a fast-acting crew can save a ship that has been torpedoed. Two torpedoes struck the *California* and six hit the *West Virginia*, yet neither ship capsized because their crews had time to employ counterflooding. When a torpedo pierces a ship's hull, the punctured compartment fills with water. Several flooded compartments on one side of a ship can cause it to roll and sink. But by filling compartments on the opposite side of the ship with water, the crew can even out the weight, and the ship will go straight down instead of tipping and capsizing. Although the hulls of the *California* and *West Virginia* rested on the ocean floor, the decks remained above the waterline.

## AMERICAN MUNITIONS

In part, the Japanese were able to do so much damage during this first wave of the attack because the US forces were unprepared to defend themselves. American navy ships were at a "Condition 3," a state of alert in which only a portion of any ship's guns are manned. In the case of Pearl Harbor, only one-quarter of the antiaircraft guns and none of the larger five-inch (13 cm) guns were manned.[6] Even the manned machine guns were only marginally useful because the ammunition was stored in locked boxes with the keys located elsewhere.

The situation was no better with the army antiaircraft guns located on the coast. Although there were 12 antiaircraft installations in the area, few crews were on duty on Sundays. And again, ammunition was inaccessible, stored in remote depots.

The Japanese attack destroyed several US planes at Wheeler Field, approximately ten miles (16 km) north of Pearl Harbor.

The US Army and Navy had been caught unprepared, yet various large guns had managed to down a few Japanese aircraft. American losses had been far greater, but the men were determined to fight back if the enemy returned.

# PEARL HARBOR
## SHIPS AT ANCHOR DURING THE ATTACK

Many types of ships were in Pearl Harbor on the morning of the attack, including the following:

**AMMUNITION SHIPS**

**CARGO SHIPS**

**COMBAT VESSELS**

ranging from fast-moving cruisers to larger, heavily armed destroyers, battleships, and submarines.

**HOSPITAL SHIPS**

**MINELAYERS**

for placing chained mines in the water

## MINESWEEPERS

for finding and destroying chained mines

## PATROL GUNBOATS

## OCEAN TUGS

for pushing other ships into place

## OILERS

for refueling ships at sea

## STORES ISSUE SHIPS

for carrying supplies into noncombat areas

## SUBMARINE RESCUE SHIPS

## REPAIR SHIPS AND TENDERS

ranging from destroyer tenders to submarine and seaplane tenders, each of which provided maintenance to its assigned type of ship, with repair ships fixing the most difficult problems such as damage from battle

Airmen on Ford Island watch the explosion of the USS Shaw during the second wave of

CHAPTER

**7**

# THE SECOND WAVE OF AIRCRAFT

When the first wave of Japanese aircraft flew back to the carriers, the Americans did not know what was going to happen next. But the men were trained to fight, and they prepared to do just that.

## 8:40 A.M.

The *Nevada* had not been docked among the other battleships, and its crew already had two boilers going. The boilers provided steam to power the ship; because the boilers were hot, the ship had power to get under way. It was the only battleship to do so. Its crew cast off, and the *Nevada* moved toward the harbor's entrance in an attempt to move into the open sea where the ship would have more room to maneuver.

## 8:54 A.M.

Before the *Nevada* cleared the mouth of the harbor, the second wave of Japanese aircraft—35 fighters, 78 dive bombers, and 54 high-altitude bombers—reached Oahu.[1] The sight of the *Nevada* motoring across the harbor attracted the attention of the Japanese pilots, who had been told to bomb any fleeing ships. Dive bombers struck the *Nevada* with six bombs even as its crew opened fire, taking down four or five enemy aircraft.[2] Worried the ship would sink and block the entrance of the harbor, the control tower ordered the crew to beach the *Nevada*. The crew ran the ship aground at Hospital Point.

The Japanese bombers also attacked the navy yard dry dock, the maintenance area where ships are removed from the water for repair. When a bomb hit a pair of oil tanks, the explosion ignited ammunition stores on the destroyer *Cassin*, which then rolled off its blocks into a second destroyer, the *Downes*. Another bomb hit and damaged the battleship *Pennsylvania*.

The Japanese pilots in the second wave also targeted airfields to destroy long-range aircraft such as those based at Hickam Field. If left undestroyed, these American planes could have followed the Japanese pilots back to their fleet

## THE CHEER UP SHIP

All naval ships are given nicknames by their crews. The *Nevada* was called the "Cheer Up Ship." The day after the attack on Pearl Harbor, Vice Admiral Lorenzo S. Sabin visited a wreck that was anything but cheery. He later described the main deck as covered in twisted bloody steel. Men worked to pull "bodies and parts of bodies" from the wreckage. By the next day, all debris was gone and the deck had been washed clean. Men had hung up signs painted with slogans such as "We'll fight again" and "Cheer up the Cheer Up Ship."[3]

Two men investigate the damage at Hickam Field, where Japanese bombs destroyed hangars and several planes.

and attacked the vulnerable aircraft carriers. During this assault, Hickam Field lost aircraft, hangars, and the barracks.

The second attack did not do as much damage as the first, in part because of the type of aircraft Japan used. The first attack had been carried out largely by torpedo bombers, which dropped torpedoes that easily penetrated the ships'

The USS *Shaw*, a destroyer, explodes after being attacked by Japanese dive bombers. The ship was repaired after the attack and went on to serve in the Pacific until 1945.

hulls. However, thick smoke billowed from the fires that had been burning since the first attack, and this reduced visibility throughout the harbor. Because of this, the Japanese primarily used their more maneuverable dive bombers during the second attack. But the dive bombers' small bombs failed to penetrate the American ships' heavy armor.

## FLYING BLIND

Most modern aircraft come equipped with radar so the pilots can locate other planes and ships. Japanese fighters had no radar and no homing devices. To make their way back to the fleet, they had to meet up with the Japanese bombers and follow these larger planes back to the carriers.

The high-altitude planes attacking the airfields used much larger bomb loads that could cause substantial damage. However, the high-altitude bombers carrying these payloads were not as accurate as the dive bombers or torpedo bombers. The Japanese also did less damage during this part of the attack because, without the element of surprise, they faced resistance.

## THE UNITED STATES FIGHTS BACK

From the beginning of the first wave, US soldiers, sailors, and pilots scrambled to prepare their aircraft and guns so they could fight back. After fueling and arming their Curtis P-36 Hawks, four pilots at Wheeler Field took off even as the bombs of the second wave dropped around them.[4]

After the pilots climbed to 9,000 feet (2,700 m), they saw Japanese dive bombers and attacked.[5] Lieutenant Lewis Sanders got on the tail of a bomber and gunned it down. Lieutenant Gordon Sterling shot down another Japanese plane, but his own plane was downed at sea and he was killed.

## ORDINARY DAY

In the 1940s, radio was a popular form of entertainment, and people listened to news programming, radio dramas, and music. With no Internet or text messaging, news about important events did not spread as quickly as it does today. That meant most people had a typical Sunday afternoon before they heard about the Pearl Harbor bombing. Many New Yorkers were listening to the 3:00 p.m. radio broadcast of the New York Philharmonic Orchestra.[7] During the intermission, CBS announcer John Charles Daly reported that the Japanese had bombed Pearl Harbor approximately three hours earlier.

The guns on Lieutenant Philip M. Rasmussen's plane started firing even though Rasmussen had not pulled the trigger. As he attempted to get his weapons under control, a Japanese plane flew in front of him and exploded. Rasmussen's plane later got hit by a Japanese fighter, and he had to crash-land his plane.

Approximately six pilots made it into the air during the second wave of the attack. Between them and the antiaircraft guns other men had armed and operated, the United States shot down 20 Japanese aircraft.[6]

When radar operators had spotted the first flight of Japanese planes approaching Oahu, the Combat Information Center was understaffed. Only one officer was on duty, and because of his inexperience he did not appreciate the significance of the flight radar reading. By the end of the attack, the center was fully staffed, but it still failed to track the retreating Japanese aircraft back to the fleet. This allowed the Japanese force to once again disappear from sight.

## JAPANESE FAILURES

As successful as the combined Japanese attacks had been, they failed in several key areas. First, and most important, the US aircraft carriers had not been in the

People pick through the wreckage of a plane after the attack is over.

harbor. On November 28, Kimmel had sent the USS *Enterprise* to Wake Island
with 12 fighter planes for the marines stationed there. On December 5, the USS
*Lexington* had left Pearl Harbor for Midway with 18 aircraft for another group of
marines.[8] The USS *Saratoga* was in California, where it had just been overhauled
and was preparing to sail back to Pearl Harbor. Because these ships were not

The USS *Enterprise*, which was not in Pearl Harbor during the attack, went on to earn present, the Japanese pilots did not have the opportunity to destroy these valuable targets.

The Japanese also failed to destroy the fuel tanks and repair shops of the naval shipyard. Although the dry docks had suffered damage, the facilities were largely intact, so repairs could begin immediately on at least some of the damaged ships.

Finally, the Japanese also failed to destroy the US submarine base, which became important later in the war as US submarines hunted down Japanese subs. At the time of the attack, four US subs, the *Cachalot,* the *Dolphin,* the *Narwhal,* and the *Tautog,* were docked in the submarine base.[9] At the base for repair, they were all partially dismantled and unable to submerge, yet none of them were damaged.

With aircraft carriers and submarines as well as a working repair facility, the United States was poised to rebound into a style of warfare not seen before—in the air and under the waves, not just on the surface of the sea.

People rush to buy newspapers to learn about the Japanese attack.

# THE AFTERMATH

At Hickam Station Hospital, two nurses were the only medical staff on duty when the attack began. They heard a thud as a bomb struck the hospital lawn. This was the first time American women who served as military nurses were on the front lines. In previous wars, they had been at evacuation hospitals miles away from the battle itself.

The wounded had to be treated immediately after the attack, as men brought their fellow soldiers and sailors—burned, shot, and wounded by shrapnel—to the hospitals. These hospitals quickly filled with men lining the halls and stairwells. Nurses and doctors treated the injured on lawns and in improvised hospitals set up in barracks, dining halls, and schools.

Army regulations required that hospital supplies be kept under lock and key, similar to the situation with munitions. Therefore, certain important items were hard to access. Even supplies that were quickly used up in an emergency had to be restocked through specific bureaucratic steps. Because of this, doctors and nurses found themselves using cleaning rags as face masks and performing surgery without gloves.

Many nurses had only morphine to ease their patients' pain and suffering. Without the normal charts and paperwork to let other medical personnel know which patients had been given this powerful painkiller, nurses improvised by writing a lipstick *M* on the forehead of each medicated man. The medical staff struggled to save as many injured men as possible.

## REPAIRING THE DAMAGE

Following the attack, Pearl Harbor was a "chaotic soup of violently rent metal, oily water, trapped poisonous gases, unexploded ordnance, and debris of every imaginable form, including human bodies."[1] Despite the chaos, the soldiers and sailors got to work to put their ships and aircraft back into working order.

Because the harbor was only 30 to 40 feet (9 to 12 m) deep, sunk ships were not completely submerged.[2] The first step in repairing damaged ships was to pump out water and raise them to the surface. After closing a ship's doors and

## SUPER RACISM

One of the tools used to create support for the US military effort—as well as hatred and distrust of the enemy—was propaganda. Propaganda is a method of affecting people's emotions by spreading positive or negative ideas about a certain topic. Posters sported slogans, and comic books contained stories of sabotage and spies. Much of this propaganda was racist. Japanese soldiers were often shown with devilishly pointed ears and teeth. In other instances, they were shown as monkeys with Japanese faces. Many Americans found it easier to think of the Japanese as enemies if they were not entirely human.

creating blockages with concrete, men pumped air into the ship. These interior air bubbles helped raise the ship while water was pumped out. In some cases, fuel oil and ammunition had to be removed before repairs could begin. When necessary, ships were pulled upright and then holes were sealed. Only then were sections of decking and hulls cut away so new material could be welded and riveted into place.

Of the eight battleships that were severely damaged, all but two went on to fight in the war. Several were back in service just weeks after the attack; others took longer to repair, but extensive work made it possible to update the ships. The *West Virginia* did not rejoin the fleet until 1944, but it did so with a sleek, modern structure, heavier antiaircraft guns, and the latest radar systems.

The ships and aircraft damaged at Pearl Harbor were all old, and many in the military considered them obsolete. Repair work, along with the construction of replacement ships and aircraft, allowed the United States to modernize its aging equipment to fight in the upcoming war.

## ROSIE THE RIVETER

In addition to using propaganda campaigns to stir up public support for the military and the war, the US government also used these campaigns to influence where people worked. The Rosie the Riveter campaign recruited women for the defense industry. According to the propaganda, women should not work simply to help feed their families; it was their patriotic duty to take on jobs normally done by men so the men could go off and fight.

## PANIC ON THE MAINLAND

Japan's military advisers intended for the Pearl Harbor attack to so dishearten the American people that the United States would be unable to make a comeback.

This demoralization, as well as the destruction of the US fleet, would keep the United States out of the war.

The attack did shock people, and they turned to President Roosevelt for comfort. The night of the bombing, crowds gathered around the White House. Some people stood against the iron fence surrounding the White House, while others waited in Lafayette Park across the street. People watched and waited for some sign from the president.

US officials worried about which military or government target would be hit next. Measures were immediately taken to keep the president safe from Japanese aircraft. The guard on the White House was increased, and blackout curtains were hung on the building's windows. Soldiers even placed antiaircraft guns on the roof of the building next to the White House.

## DECLARATION OF WAR

The day after the attack on Pearl Harbor, Roosevelt gave a speech to a joint congressional session asking them to declare war. In this speech, he said, "Yesterday, December 7, 1941—a date which will live in infamy—the United States of America was suddenly and deliberately attacked by naval and air forces of the Empire of Japan."[3]

After the speech, it took only 30 minutes for every member of the Senate to vote for war. The House vote did not go as smoothly. Jeannette Rankin, the representative from Montana and a pacifist, said she would vote against this war just as she had voted against World War I. She was shouted down by her fellow representatives. When the vote was taken, it was 388 to 1. Rankin was the only member of Congress to vote against war.[4]

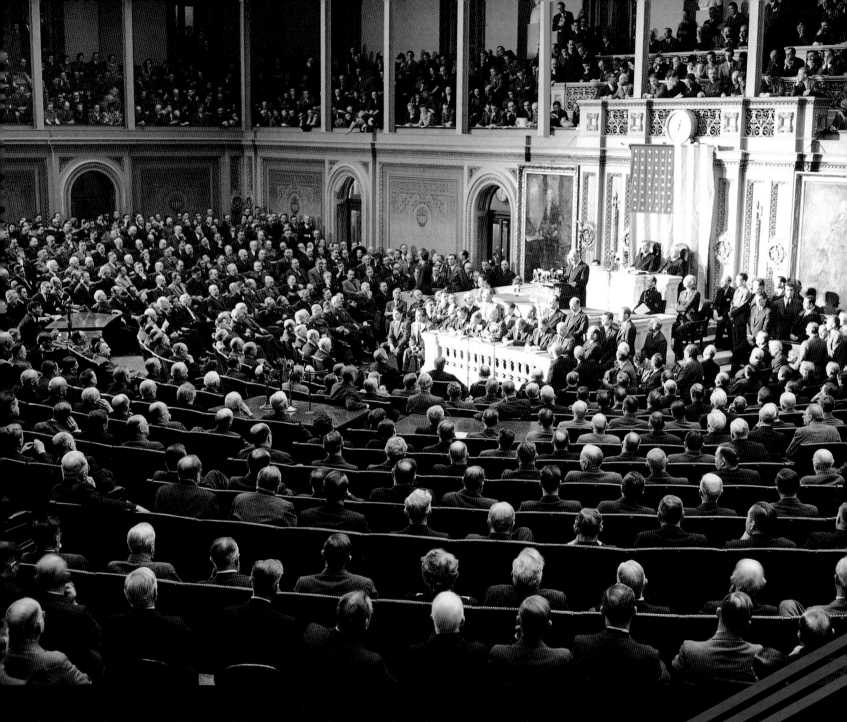
President Roosevelt addressed Congress on December 8, 1941

Although many Americans had been against war, the attack on Pearl Harbor did not demoralize the nation's people. It brought them together with a common goal: to fight back.

On both coasts, soldiers set up antiaircraft guns along docks and on rooftops. Not enough fully functional guns were available, so they used old guns and even wooden props. Many of the men who guarded weapons factories and railway stations carried outdated rifles that were more than 20 years old. Brigadier General John C. MacDonnell, an air-raid warning chief, ordered a 24-hour sky watch throughout the winter holidays. People also worried about potential nonmilitary and government targets. For example, the Rose Bowl, an important college football game, was moved from California to North Carolina.

As the Japanese predicted, fear did not dissipate quickly. However, there was one effect the Japanese may not have anticipated. The attack on Pearl Harbor spurred many Americans into action against people of Japanese descent.

## EXECUTIVE ORDER 9066

The attack on Pearl Harbor fueled racism and paranoia against Japanese Americans. People worried if the Japanese invaded the mainland, or even if they sneaked in to commit acts of sabotage, Japanese Americans living on the West Coast would aid them.

To prevent this possibility, Roosevelt signed Executive Order 9066 on February 19, 1942. This order, which affected more than 120,000 individuals, required people of Japanese ancestry to move to internment camps.[5] In these camps, entire families were held prisoner. Approximately two-thirds of those affected were Nisei, or people of Japanese descent who were born in the United

People of Japanese descent gather at an internment camp in Manzanar, California.

States, and therefore American citizens.[6] Colorado governor Ralph Lawrence Carr was the only US governor to object to this plan.

The people affected by Executive Order 9066 had only one week to sell their homes, farms, and businesses. Because so many properties were being sold at the same time, people had to accept a fraction of their properties' true value. Many people were unable to sell their property before being imprisoned.

Ten camps were built in remote areas of the United States, including the deserts of several western states. Families were forced to live in tar-paper barracks and take their meals in communal mess halls. School was provided for the children. Many adults worked, digging ditches and canals, planting and tending gardens, and raising livestock.

Interned people struggled to grow their own food, as the soil was poor and they did not have enough water. They fought to lead productive lives as prisoners of their own government. Guards kept watch in gun towers and scanned the camp boundaries for anyone trying to escape. Escapees would be shot.

After being forced to swear an oath of allegiance to the United States, many Nisei men joined the military, serving

## AFTER THE CAMPS CLOSED

When the internment camps disbanded, it was up to the internees to restart their lives. Those who had not sold their property returned home, often to discover that someone else had moved onto their land and had to be evicted. Others reached their hometowns and found signs that warned them away, such as "No Japs Wanted"[7] and "We Don't Want Any Japs Back Here . . . Ever!"[8] Others came out of the camps with little or no money to begin new lives. Yet they did, working hard to take advantage of whatever opportunities they could find.

# RALPH LAWRENCE CARR

## 1887–1950

Colorado governor Ralph Lawrence Carr was one of a small number of politicians who objected to the relocation of the Japanese. "If we do not protect and preserve the Constitution and the Bill of Rights for all men today," he said, "it will not serve as a protection for any man six months from now."[9]

Before the war, people thought Carr would have a career in national politics. He declined an invitation to run as the vice-presidential candidate under Republican nominee Wendell Willkie, and he was identified in various newspapers as a possible presidential candidate. All of that ended when Carr denounced the internment camps. Instead of a potential president, he was called "Jap Lover," and he lost his bid for a US Senate seat in 1942.

Following his death, Carr was honored with plaques and memorials and a highway named after him. But when he was alive, Carr stood alone when he spoke up in support of Japanese Americans.

in the European theater. Their unit, the army's combined 100/442 Combat Team, rescued an American infantry division in the forests of France, made two beachhead assaults in France and Italy, and captured an enemy submarine. The team also opened the gates of Dachau concentration camp in Germany. The team's insignia was the hand of Lady Liberty holding high the torch of freedom.

## UNCLE SAM WANTS YOU

On September 16, 1940, more than a year before the attack on Pearl Harbor, the United States had instituted the country's first peacetime draft. This draft required all men aged 21 to 36 to register. Although the United States was not at war, Roosevelt had watched the Germans invade countries in Europe and the Japanese do the same in Asia. Americans may not have wanted to get involved, but if war came, Roosevelt and Congress wanted the United States to be ready. The draft resulted in the registration of 36 million men. Six thousand local draft boards, located in cities and towns across the country, examined each man and decided whether he was fit to serve.[10] The decision was based on how important his job was to the war effort, his individual health, and his family situation. Even in a time of war, men had to pass an array of physical and mental tests before being chosen to serve as a soldier, pilot, or sailor.

The US military was not made up entirely of draftees. Many men, and some women, volunteered to serve. These volunteers got to choose which branch of the military they joined. In contrast, most draftees were placed in the army, with some in the navy and only a small number in the marines.

After joining the military, the new recruits had to go through training camps. At these camps, they underwent rigorous physical conditioning, learned how to work as part of a team, and learned how to handle a variety of weapons. Whether someone was a cook, a driver, or a clerk, he was first and foremost a soldier.

Testing also helped the military identify who had the skills needed for a wide variety of jobs. These men went on to receive additional training at centers devoted specifically to desert troops, antiaircraft groups, and paratroopers who dropped from aircraft. However, expanding the military was not just a matter of finding people to do various jobs.

## WARTIME ECONOMY

As the military added new soldiers, sailors, and pilots, the rest of the country geared up to produce the materials these new military men and women needed, such as uniforms, guns, tanks, ships, and planes. The military needed these items

A propaganda poster urges Americans to join the fight against the Japanese.

as fast as possible, so manufacturers retooled factories to produce war goods. For example, in February 1942, manufacturer Fisher Body switched from making bodies for cars to bodies for Sherman tanks. Pontiac, a carmaker, started making front axles for M-5 tanks. Buick, another carmaker, retooled its Melrose Park factory to make casings for ammunition and build engines for the B-24 bomber.

## CIVILIANS AT WAR

As more resources were funneled toward the military, civilians had to work with less. Some items were rationed, meaning a person could buy only a limited amount and had to have a government coupon to get it. Rationed food items included sugar, meat, and coffee. "Victory cookbooks" offered housewives advice on how to make rationed goods go as far as possible. With so much of farmers' harvests going to feed soldiers, civilians planted Victory gardens, growing vegetables and fruit in backyards, vacant lots, and parks. These gardens produced an estimated 1 million tons (0.9 metric tons) of food during the war.[11]

The war also affected travel because so many tires were needed for military jeeps, trucks, and planes. The rubber to make US tires had come from Southeast Asia, which was now under Japanese control. Gas rationing, speed limits, and car pool programs all worked to limit wear and tear on the nation's tires.

In addition to rationing, many items were recycled, including rags, silk, and string. Aluminum and steel were recycled to be made into canteens, ammunition, and ships. People salvaged cars, bed frames, radiators, pots, and pipes. Even fat was recycled so it could be used to make glycerin for ammunition. Together, Americans gathered the material needed to help US soldiers, pilots, and sailors win the war.

Retooling plants helped get production started, but it was not enough to produce everything that was needed. Therefore, new factories were built all over the country. Ford Motor Company built the Willow Run bomber plant for the assembly of the B-24 Liberator.

By 1944, US factories were building almost 100,000 aircraft a year.[12] Factories accomplished this feat by working efficiently and often running their lines around the clock. The Willow Run bomber factory produced almost one plane every hour. Americans were taking production to levels that few people had believed possible.

Before the war, there had been more people than jobs, but now anyone who wanted a job could find one. Factories running long hours required more workers, and the government and industry encouraged women to enter the workforce. Some women stayed in the low-paying jobs they had had before the war, such as teaching, secretarial work, and waitressing—but many took jobs in the defense industry, shipbuilding, and aircraft manufacturing. Though these jobs paid women more than the jobs they had had before the war, they still made less than men made doing the same jobs. At the end of the war in late 1945, when the soldiers returned home, women were expected to leave the factories and give up their jobs.

Pearl Harbor pulled the United States into a war many people had worked hard to avoid. Voters may have elected Roosevelt because he promised to keep them out of the war, but once the war had begun, Americans worked together to win.

# TIMELINE

**1853**
Commodore Perry sails into Tokyo Bay.

**1931**
Japan invades Manchuria.

**July 1940**
Japanese troops move into Indochina.

**September 2, 1940**
The United States gives the United Kingdom 50 US destroyers in exchange for military bases in the North Atlantic.

**November 26, 1941**
Japanese aircraft carriers and other warships leave Japan for Pearl Harbor.

**November 27, 1941**
US Admiral Harold Stark warns that "hostile action possible at any moment."

**November 28, 1941**
The carrier USS *Enterprise* leaves Pearl Harbor for Wake Island.

**December 5, 1941**
The carrier USS *Lexington* leaves Pearl Harbor for Midway.

**September 16, 1940**

The United States institutes its first peacetime military draft.

**September 27, 1940**

Germany, Italy, and Japan sign the Tripartite Pact and become allies.

**October 1940**

The US government halts the export of oil and steel to Japan.

**January 1941**

Admiral Isoroku Yamamoto begins planning Japan's attack on Pearl Harbor.

**December 7, 1941**

Japan attacks Pearl Harbor.

**December 8, 1941**

The United States declares war on Japan.

**February 19, 1942**

Executive Order 9066 requires people of Japanese ancestry to move to internment camps.

**1945**

US soldiers begin returning home, and women are forced back out of wartime jobs.

# ESSENTIAL FACTS

## KEY PLAYERS

- Mitsuo Fuchida coordinates Japan's aerial attack on Pearl Harbor and leads the first wave.

- Admiral Husband E. Kimmel of the US Navy is serving as commander in chief of the US Pacific Fleet at the time of the attack.

- General George Marshall is chief of staff of the US Army and a primary military adviser to President Roosevelt.

- Franklin Delano Roosevelt is president of the United States.

- Lieutenant General Walter Campbell Short serves in the US Army and is responsible for military defense in Hawaii.

- Admiral Isoroku Yamamoto is the commander of Japan's combined fleet and a key planner for the attack on Pearl Harbor.

## KEY STATISTICS

- The Japanese attacks damage eight battleships.

- A total of 188 US aircraft are destroyed in the attack.

- 2,403 Americans are killed in the Pearl Harbor attack.

- 64 Japanese pilots and sailors die during the attack.

## IMPACT ON THE WAR

The attack on Pearl Harbor leads the United States to immediately declare war on Japan. In response, Japan's allies Germany and Italy declare war on the United States. The attack thus brings the United States into both the Pacific and European theaters of war. American production and manpower prove decisive factors in the war's outcome.

## IMPACT ON SOCIETY

Because of the Pearl Harbor attack and fears of a second attack aided by resident Japanese, more than 120,000 people of Japanese descent in the United States are imprisoned at camps set up throughout the country. Two-thirds of them are US citizens. Pearl Harbor also leads to the buildup of the US military and the industry needed to supply this military. These increases in industry pull the United States out of the Great Depression.

## QUOTE

"Yesterday, December 7, 1941—a date which will live in infamy—the United States of America was suddenly and deliberately attacked by naval and air forces of the Empire of Japan."

—*Franklin Delano Roosevelt*

# GLOSSARY

**CALL SIGN**
A radio message or code used to identify the sender or the location.

**COMMISSION**
To put a ship into service.

**DEPTH CHARGE**
A bomb that explodes when it reaches a certain depth underwater.

**DIPLOMAT**
A person appointed to act for his or her government in another country, often an ambassador or a staff member from an embassy.

**FLAGSHIP**
The ship that carries the highest-ranking officer in a fleet.

**GREAT DEPRESSION**
A worldwide period of economic depression in the 1930s. In a depression, large numbers of people are out of work, many people lose their homes, and many businesses fail.

**INTERNMENT**
Confinement or imprisonment.

## KEEL

Part of the central structure of a ship. The floor and frames attach to the keel.

## MISSIONARY

A church employee who is sent to another country to teach others about the church or to operate a school or hospital.

## MOORING BUOY

A large float to which ships are tied to anchor them in place.

## OFFICER OF THE DAY

The officer who works, for that day, under the commanding officer to make sure things run smoothly.

## OSCILLOSCOPE

An instrument that measures changes in electrical signals.

## PACIFIST

A person who is against war or violence.

## SUPERSTRUCTURE

The parts of a ship that are above the main deck that are also a continuation of the sides of the ship.

# ADDITIONAL RESOURCES

## SELECTED BIBLIOGRAPHY

Gillon, Steven M. *Pearl Harbor: FDR Leads the Nation into War*. New York: Basic, 2011. Print.

Mawdsley, Evan. *December 1941: Twelve Days That Began a World War*. New Haven: Yale UP, 2011. Print.

Scott, James. *The War Below: The Story of Three Submarines That Battled Japan*. New York: Simon, 2013. Print.

## FURTHER READINGS

Haugen, David, and Susan Musser. *The Attack on Pearl Harbor*. Detroit: Greenhaven, 2011. Print.

Hoyt, Edwin P. *Pearl Harbor Attack*. New York: Sterling, 2008. Print.

Stille, Mark E. *Tora! Tora! Tora! Pearl Harbor 1941*. Long Island City, NY: Osprey, 2011. Print.

Woog, Adam. *Pearl Harbor*. San Diego, CA: ReferencePoint, 2013. Print.

## WEBSITES

To learn more about Essential Library of World War II, visit **booklinks.abdopublishing.com**. These links are routinely monitored and updated to provide the most current information available.

## PLACES TO VISIT

**Battleship Missouri Memorial**
63 Cowpens Street
Honolulu, HI 96818
808-455-1600
https://ussmissouri.org
This site is significant because the Japanese signed the treaty of surrender on the *Missouri*.

**Pacific Aviation Museum**
319 Lexington Boulevard
Honolulu, HI 96818
808-441-1000
http://www.pacificaviationmuseum.org
This museum is dedicated to the various aircraft, pilots, and support personnel who defended the Pacific.

**World War II Valor in the Pacific National Monument**
1 Arizona Memorial Place
Honolulu, HI 96818
808-422-3399
http://www.nps.gov/valr/index.htm
Located in Pearl Harbor, this museum presents information about the war in the Pacific including Pearl Harbor.

# SOURCE NOTES

## CHAPTER 1. WAR COMES TO THE UNITED STATES

1. Robert S. LaForte and Ronald E. Marcello, eds. *Remembering Pearl Harbor: Eyewitness Accounts by US Military Men and Women*. New York: Ballantine, 1991. Print. 27–28.

2. Ibid. 28–29.

3. "Pearl Harbor Time Line." *National Geographic*. National Geographic Society, 2001. Web. 20 Mar. 2015.

4. "Pearl Harbor: Day of Infamy." *Military.com*. Military Advantage, n.d. Web. 20 Mar. 2015.

5. "USS *Arizona* History." *PearlHarbor.org*. PearlHarbor.org, n.d. Web. 20 Mar. 2015.

6. D. Clayton James and Anne Sharp Wells. *From Pearl Harbor to V-J Day: The American Armed Forces in World War II*. Chicago: I. R. Dee, 1995. Print. 116.

## CHAPTER 2. GLOBAL UNREST

1. John K. Fairbank, Edwin O. Reischauer, and Albert M. Craig. *East Asia: Tradition and Transformation*. Boston: Houghton, 1978. Print. 517.

2. Lynne Olson. *Those Angry Days: Roosevelt, Lindbergh, and America's Fight over World War II, 1939–1941*. New York: Random, 2013. Print. 54.

3. "People & Events: Emperor Hirohito (1901–1989)." *American Experience*. PBS, n.d. Web. 20 Mar. 2015.

4. "WWI Casualty and Death Tables." *PBS*. PBS, n.d. Web. 20 Mar. 2015.

5. Lynne Olson. *Those Angry Days: Roosevelt, Lindbergh, and America's Fight over World War II, 1939–1941*. New York: Random, 2013. Print. 34.

6. Jon Thares Davidann. *Cultural Diplomacy in US–Japanese Relations, 1919–1941*. New York: Palgrave, 2007. Print. 180.

7. Ibid.

8. "Franklin D. Roosevelt." *History.com*. A&E Television Networks, n.d. Web. 20 Mar. 2015.

9. John W. Dower. *Cultures of War: Pearl Harbor/Hiroshima/9-11/Iraq*. New York: Norton, 2010. Print. 24.

## CHAPTER 3. JAPAN'S PLAN

1. Scot MacDonald. *Evolution of Aircraft Carriers.* Washington, DC: US Navy, October 1962. 39. *Naval History and Heritage Command.* Web. 20 Mar. 2015.

2. Ibid. 40.

3. Ibid. 42.

4. Robert J. Hanyok. "Catching the Fox Unaware: Japanese Radio Denial and Deception and the Attack on Pearl Harbor." *Naval War College Review* 61.4. (2008): 102. Print.

## CHAPTER 4. LIMITED INTELLIGENCE

1. Stephen Budiansky. *Battle of Wits: The Complete Story of Codebreaking in World War II.* New York: Free Press, 2000. Print. 319.

2. Steve Horn. *The Second Attack on Pearl Harbor: Operation K and Other Japanese Attempts to Bomb America in World War II.* Annapolis, MD: Naval Institute, 2005. Print. 171.

3. Paul S. Burtness and Warren U. Ober. "Communication Lapses Leading to the Pearl Harbor Disaster." *The Historian* 75.4 (2013): 745. Print.

4. William M. Cahill. "Technology Not Realized: Army Air Forces Radar Employment in the Early Pacific War." *Air Power History* 56.2 (2009). Print.

5. Ibid.

6. Richard Goldstein. "Kermit Tyler, Player of a Fateful, if Minor, Role in Pearl Harbor Attack, Dies at 96." *New York Times.* New York Times, 25 Feb. 2010. Web. 20 Mar. 2015.

# SOURCE NOTES
## CONTINUED

### CHAPTER 5. SUBMARINES

1. Gordon W. Prange, Donald M. Goldstein, and Katherine V. Dillon. *Pearl Harbor: The Verdict of History*. New York: Penguin, 1991. Print.

2. "Japanese Submarine Sunk at Pearl Harbor Is Found." *New York Times*. New York Times, 30 Aug. 2002. Web. 20 Mar. 2015.

3. Thomas H. Maugh II. "Pearl Harbor Mini-Submarine Mystery Solved?" *Los Angeles Times*. Los Angeles Times, 7 Dec. 2009. Web. 20 Mar. 2015.

4. "Pearl Harbor Time Line." *National Geographic*. National Geographic Society, 2001. Web. 20 Mar. 2015.

5. Burl Burlingame. "Anatomy of a Secret Sub." *Honolulu Star-Bulletin*. Honolulu Star-Bulletin, 1 Sep. 2002. Web. 20 Mar. 2015.

### CHAPTER 6. THE FIRST WAVE OF AIRCRAFT

1. Mark Stille. "Yamamoto and the Planning for Pearl Harbor." *The History Reader*. The History Reader, 26 Nov. 2012. Web. 20 Mar. 2015.

2. "Pearl Harbor Time Line." *National Geographic*. National Geographic Society, 2001. Web. 20 Mar. 2015.

3. Evan Mawdsley. *December 1941: Twelve Days that Began a World War*. New Haven, CT: Yale UP, 2011. Print. 171.

4. Ibid. 172.

5. Ibid. 173.

6. Ibid. 172.

### CHAPTER 7. THE SECOND WAVE OF AIRCRAFT

1. "Pearl Harbor Time Line." *National Geographic*. National Geographic Society, 2001. Web. 20 Mar. 2015.

2. Ibid.

3. Paul Stillwell, ed. *Air Raid, Pearl Harbor!: Recollections of a Day of Infamy*. Annapolis, MD: Naval Institute, 1981. Print. 146.

4. Robert F. Dorr. "Pearl Harbor: The Army Air Forces Fight Back." *Defense Media Network*. Faircount Media Group, 7 Dec. 2011. Web. 20 Mar. 2015.

5. Ibid.

6. Robert F. Dorr. "The Few Who Got Up." *Defense Media Network*. Faircount Media Group, 22 Oct. 2009. Web. 20 Mar. 2015.

7. Lynne Olson. *Those Angry Days: Roosevelt, Lindbergh, and America's Fight over World War II, 1939–1941*. New York: Random, 2013. Print. 424.

8. "Carrier Locations." *Naval History and Heritage Command*. US Navy, n.d. Web. 20 Mar. 2015.

9. "Submarines in Pearl Harbor on December 7, 1941." *USS Bowfin Submarine Museum and Park*. USS Bowfin Submarine Museum and Park, n.d. Web. 20 Mar. 2015.

## CHAPTER 8. THE AFTERMATH

1. Karen Jensen. "Rebuilding Pearl." *World War II* 22.4 (2007): 43–44. Print.

2. John Mueller. "Pearl Harbor: Military Inconvenience, Political Disaster." *International Security* 16.3 (1991): 176. Print.

3. "FDR's 'Day of Infamy' Speech: Crafting a Call to Arms." *National Archives*. National Archives, n.d. Web. 20 Mar. 2015.

4. Lynne Olson. *Those Angry Days: Roosevelt, Lindbergh, and America's Fight over World War II, 1939–1941*. New York: Random, 2013. Print. 429–30.

5. "Civil Rights: Japanese Americans." *The War*. PBS, n.d. Web. 20 Mar. 2015.

6. "Japanese-American Internment." *USHistory.org*. Independence Hall Association, n.d. Web. 20 Mar. 2015.

7. Jane McGrath. "Did the United States Put Its Own Citizens in Concentration Camps during World War II?" *HowStuffWorks.com*. InfoSpace, n.d. Web. 20 Mar. 1015.

8. *This is the Enemy*. Dir. Gretchen Jahn Bertram. *Ohio State University eHistory*. Web. 20 Mar. 2015.

9. Adam Schrager. *The Principled Politician: The Ralph Carr Story*. Golden, CO: Fulcrum, 2008. Print. 238.

10. "America Goes to War." *The National WWII Museum*. The National WWII Museum, n.d. Web. 20 Mar. 2015.

11. "Victory Gardens at a Glance." *The National WWII Museum*. The National WWII Museum, n.d. Web. 20 Mar. 2015.

12. Wesley Frank Craven and James Lea Cate, eds. *The Army Air Forces in World War II, Vol. VI: Men and Planes*. Washington, DC: Office of Air Force History, 1983. Print.

# INDEX

aircraft, 30, 32, 79
    Japanese planes, 8, 11, 12, 13, 30, 32, 34, 41, 44, 53, 58, 61, 63, 64, 66, 67, 68, 71, 75, 76, 77, 79, 80, 88
    US planes, 12, 25, 41, 47, 48, 51, 64, 66, 76, 77, 79, 80, 81, 86, 87, 95, 96, 97
aircraft carriers, 13, 30, 32, 33, 34, 36, 40, 48, 63, 66, 75, 77, 79, 80, 83
*Akagi*, 30
Aleutian Islands, 41
ammunition, 8, 13, 70, 72, 76, 87, 96
*Arizona*, USS, 7, 8, 11, 13, 68
Army, US, 11, 26, 47, 70, 71, 85, 94

Battle of the Atlantic, 25
Battleship Row, 66, 68
battleships, 7, 11, 12, 40, 67, 68, 72, 75, 76, 87
blitzkrieg, 35

*California*, USS, 66, 68, 70
Carr, Ralph Lawrence, 92, 93
*Cassin*, USS, 76
casualties, 12, 13
China, 18, 19, 22, 25, 26, 39
Chinese Communists, 19
Chinese Nationalists, 19, 26
civilians, 12, 47, 96
coded messages, 12, 36, 37, 43–45, 51, 67

colonies, 18, 20
*Condor*, USS, 56
cruisers, 12, 30, 72

destroyers, 12, 24, 56, 58, 72, 76
Destroyers for Bases Agreement, 24–25
*Downes*, USS, 76
draft, 94
Dutch East Indies, 18, 20

*Enterprise*, USS, 81
Executive Order 9066, 90, 92

First Air Fleet, 33, 34
Ford Island, 11, 12, 66
Ford Island Command Center, 12
Ford Island Naval Air Station, 7, 8
France, 18, 20, 24, 36, 94
Fuchida, Mitsuo, 64

Germany, 20, 23, 24, 25, 26, 35, 58, 94
Great Depression, 22, 23

*Helm*, USS, 56, 69
Hickam Field, 64, 76, 77
Hirohito, 18, 20
Honolulu, Hawaii, 7, 48, 67
Hopper, Hedda, 24
*Hōshō*, 30
hospitals, 85

Imperial Diet, 18
Imperial Japanese Navy, 29, 30, 32, 33, 34, 35, 36, 37, 43, 51, 54, 67
Indochina, 18, 20, 36
Inland Sea, 39
internment camps, 90, 92, 93
Italy, 20, 26, 94

Japan, 13, 17, 18, 19–20, 29, 37, 67, 88
    alliance with Germany and Italy, 20, 26, 35
    expansion into Asia, 19–20, 22, 25–26, 36, 94, 96
    failures at Pearl Harbor, 80–81, 83
    losses at Pearl Harbor, 13
    military planning, 29–34, 36, 37
    negotiation with the United States, 39, 47
    resources, 18, 19, 20
    surrender, 58
    trade with the United States, 26

Kimmel, Husband, 45, 47, 48, 56, 66, 81

Lend-Lease, 25
*Lexington*, USS, 81

Manchuria, 19
Mao Zedong, 19
Mariana Islands, 29

Marshall, George, 44, 48
Matthews, Martin, 7–8, 11–13, 68
Midway Atoll, 41
*Monaghan*, USS, 58, 69

Nagumo, Chūichi, 40, 64
National Legion of Mothers of
  America, 24
Navy, US, 8, 12, 26, 29, 34, 35, 39,
  40, 45, 47, 53, 60, 63, 67, 70, 71,
  76, 94
Navy General Staff, 34
Netherlands, 18, 20
*Nevada*, USS, 68, 75, 76
Nimitz, Chester, 60
Nye, Gerald P., 22

*Oklahoma*, USS, 60, 66
Opana Radar Site, 48, 53

*Pennsylvania*, USS, 76
Perry, Matthew, 17, 18
Philippines, 25, 29, 32, 37
Plan Orange, 29–30
Poland, 20
propaganda, 86, 87

racism, 86, 90
radio operators, 36–37, 39, 45
radio signals, 36–37, 40, 41, 44

Ramsey, Logan C., 12
Rankin, Jeannette, 88
Roosevelt, Franklin D., 20, 22, 23,
  24, 25, 37, 44, 88, 90, 94, 97
Roosevelt, Theodore, 23
Rosie the Riveter, 87
Russia, 18

sabotage, 47, 48, 66, 86, 90
*Saratoga*, USS, 81
*Shokaku*, 30, 34
Short, Walter Campbell, 45, 47, 48,
  63, 66
Sino-Japanese War, 22
Southeast Asia, 25, 26, 96
Stafford, William, 7, 8, 13
Stark, Harold Rainsford, 44, 47, 48,
  63
submarine base, 83
submarines, 25, 53, 54, 58, 60, 67,
  72, 83, 94
  Kaiten-class miniature
    submarine, 54
  midget submarines, 13, 53, 54,
    56, 57, 58, 60, 61, 63, 69
  Sentoku submarine, 58
  transport submarines, 53, 54
Sun Yat-sen, 19

teenagers, 7, 8
Tenno. *See* Hirohito
Tokyo Bay, 17
torpedo planes, 64, 66, 68, 77, 79
torpedoes, 8, 40, 53, 54, 56, 57,
    58, 60, 66, 68, 70, 77
  Type 97, 60
trade, 17, 18, 25, 39
Tripartite Pact, 20, 26

Ultras, 44–45, 48, 67
United Kingdom, 18, 24, 25

*Ward*, USS, 56, 63
Washington, DC, 35, 44
*West Virginia*, USS, 60, 66, 68, 70,
  87
Wheeler Field, 64, 79
World War I, 22, 30, 88

Yamamoto, Isoroku, 33, 34, 35, 39,
  58
Yoshikawa, Takeo, 66, 67

Zeroes, 32
*Zuikaku*, 30, 34

# ABOUT THE AUTHOR

Sue Bradford Edwards writes nonfiction for children and teens, working from her home in Saint Louis, Missouri. Because her parents loved history, summer trips often involved visiting historic sites such as Cahokia Mounds, the remains of an ancient city, and Fort Davis, a frontier military outpost. She studied archaeology and history in college and worked as an archaeological illustrator, drawing funeral medallions once buried in a historic cemetery in Saint Louis. Her writing for young readers covers a wide range of topics including science, horses, and history. To find out more about her current writing projects, visit her blog, One Writer's Journey, at http://suebe.wordpress.com.